Interpreting Slavery at Museums and Historic Sites

INTERPRETING HISTORY

About the Series

The American Association for State and Local History publishes the *Interpreting History* series in order to provide expert, in-depth guidance in interpretation for history professionals at museums and historic sites. The books are intended to help practioners expand their interpretation to be more inclusive of the range of American history.

Books in this series help readers:

- quickly learn about the questions surrounding a specific topic,
- introduce them to the challenges of interpreting this part of history, and
- highlight best practice examples of how interpretation has been done by different organizations.

They enable institutions to place their interpretative efforts into a larger context, despite each having a specific and often localized mission. These books serve as quick references to practical considerations, further research, and historical information.

Titles in the Series

Interpreting Native American History and Culture by Raney Bench
Interpreting the Prohibition Era by Jason D. Lantzer
Interpreting African American History and Culture at Museums and Historic Sites by Max van Balgooy
Interpreting LGBT History at Museums and Historic Sites by Susan Ferentinos
Interpreting Slavery at Museums and Historic Sites by Kristin L. Gallas and James DeWolf Perry

Interpreting Slavery at Museums and Historic Sites

Edited by Kristin L. Gallas and James DeWolf Perry

Published in cooperation with the
Tracing Center on Histories and Legacies of Slavery

ROWMAN & LITTLEFIELD
Lanham • Boulder • New York • London

Published by Rowman & Littlefield
A wholly owned subsidiary of The Rowman & Littlefield Publishing Group, Inc.
4501 Forbes Boulevard, Suite 200, Lanham, Maryland 20706
www.rowman.com

Unit A, Whitacre Mews, 26-34 Stannary Street, London SE11 4AB

British Library Cataloguing in Publication Information Available

Library of Congress Cataloging-in-Publication Data Available
ISBN: 978-0-7591-2325-0 (cloth)
ISBN: 978-0-7591-2326-7 (paper)
ISBN: 978-0-7591-2327-4 (electronic)

∞™ The paper used in this publication meets the minimum requirements of American National Standard for Information Sciences—Permanence of Paper for Printed Library Materials, ANSI/NISO Z39.48-1992.

Printed in the United States of America

Dedicated to history's long-silenced millions.

Contents

Foreword

REX M. ELLIS

BLACK ACTIVIST Henry Highland Garnet remarked in 1843, "Slavery! How much misery is comprehended in that single word? What mind is there that does not shrink from its direful effects?" This excerpt is from a speech Garnet gave at the National Negro Convention in Buffalo, New York. Garnet, a minister, was speaking powerfully at a time when such inflammatory language spoken by a black man could have cost him his life. It was a period in our nation's history when the question of slavery and the toll it was taking on the soul of America was being debated, challenged, and contested. Garnet's speech shocked the nation in its bold affront to the white community and with its blatant call to arms in the black community.

The speech contributed to tensions that had already put the nation on notice—slavery would not continue without a fight. In the first sixty years of the nineteenth century, several developments took place that had begun to resonate across the nation: Gabriel Prosser's revolt, the Haitian revolution, the American colonization movement, Nat Turner's rebellion, the work of activists such as David Walker, the rise of abolitionist societies, the Fugitive Slave Act of 1850, the Kansas-Nebraska Act, John Brown's raid on Harper's Ferry, and the publication of Harriet Beecher Stowe's *Uncle Tom's Cabin*. Collectively, these events, and others, unsettled the nation, leaving civil war as the only possible resolution.

Notwithstanding the 246-year history of African American enslavement, race continues to be America's unresolved issue. Though it is not the lightning rod it once was, it continues to be endemic. It remains deeply rooted in American culture and the American psyche. Its discussion is central to any political, social, or economic discussion regarding America's history. Try as we might, slavery continues to be a conversation still odious to many. But it is one that cannot be avoided if we are to understand America's past, grapple with America's present, and realistically plot America's future.

In our nation's museums, as you will see, it is a topic that still has not made it to "Main Street." Few museums and historical sites embrace it earnestly and forthrightly, and fewer still dedicate the time, resources, and commitment required to do it well. In spite of the dizzying number of books that continue to be written about American slavery in the twentieth and twenty-first centuries, finding one that offers best practices in interpreting and presenting the subject suggests they are "as scarce as hen's teeth."

Enter the Tracing Center, an organization dedicated to helping historic sites and museums understand the challenges, needs, and methods that can assist in the creative, responsible, and credible interpretation of slavery. They offer comprehensive methods that structure, educate, train, and develop supportive environments that can prepare audiences and, most importantly, interpreters in their efforts to tell the truth of history. There are very few who are keen to embrace discussions about slavery behind closed doors, but there is an even smaller number eager to talk about it publicly. Fewer still are those who have the ability to present such a historically difficult topic in a way that can guarantee a positive response from the dwindling audiences visiting their institutions.

Interpreting Slavery at Museums and Historic Sites is a comprehensive "how to" manual. It can be extremely useful to any historical or cultural institution serious about improving its ability to present the topic of slavery in ways that acknowledge its foundational significance in the evolution of our nation. The contributors suggest tools that will assist in planning, preparing, and presenting in ways that benefit both the educational practitioner and the visitor. This book addresses the root causes of inaction on every level, from the planning of programs and activities to the organizational support necessary to maintain a legitimate and consistent presence. Whether we label our current baseline of tolerance "postracial" or, as one contributor calls it, "unconscious racial bias," we continue to struggle with slavery. If that struggle is to continue, and ultimately expand at America's museums and historic sites, this seminal work should be on the shelf of every museum's staff library.

It is time, I would argue, to embrace new methods of interpreting slavery. Such methods should motivate dialogue, inspire interest, and challenge long-held myths in ways that move us from avoidance and name-calling to environments and presenters who are willing to tell compelling stories in dynamic ways. Professionals equipped with the proper tools and understanding will be able to interpret slavery not simply as African American history, but as the quintessential history of our nation.

Slavery should not be avoided because it is difficult or complex and makes most of us uncomfortable when talking about it. On the contrary, it is because of its complexity and its discomfort that we must continue the discussion. The contributors to *Interpreting Slavery* are dedicated to helping their readers attain such an end. I am convinced that what you are about to read will make a significant impact on you and those like you who dare to ask the question: How can I be part of the solution instead of continuing to deny that a solution is necessary?

Acknowledgments

WE ARE GRATEFUL to our contributing authors for their willingness to plunge into this project, to take editorial comments, and to seek out lessons for the field. We also offer our thanks to Bob Beatty at the American Association for State and Local History, for his enthusiasm and support, and for believing in the Tracing Center; to Max van Balgooy, our fellow author/editor in the *Interpreting* series, for his guidance in navigating the early stages of this project; and to Julia Rose, whose research into interpreting difficult histories helped to inspire our development of the framework for comprehensive and conscientious interpretation of slavery. Thanks also to Rex Ellis for pioneering the interpretation of slavery and for his support of this project. And to our colleague Marga Varea, thank you so much for holding the Tracing Center together while we devoted considerable time to this project.

From Kristin: To my parents, Donna and Michael, who took us on family vacations to historic sites along the East Coast. Your passion for history rubbed off, and your support and guidance helped steer me into a career that I love.

From James: To Sumi, for her love and her steadfast support of my work at the Tracing Center and all that it represents. I couldn't ask for anything more.

Preface

"If not us, then who? If not now, then when?"

"IF NOT US, then who? If not now, then when?" Congressman John Lewis said these words in reference to the civil rights movement of the mid-twentieth century. The same words apply, we believe, to the long-overdue interpretation of chattel slavery, in a comprehensive and conscientious manner, at historic sites and museums throughout the United States. Interpreting slavery with its powerful resonances is a privilege and a great responsibility. For many years, the field at large has neglected to interpret, interpreted incompletely, or perpetuated myths about the presence and lives of enslaved people at historic sites and museums across the country. We have an obligation to the public to share a comprehensive and conscientious story of the past, especially as studies show that the public considers museums to be their most trusted source of historical information.[1]

As historic sites and museums position themselves to bear witness to the tragic history of US slavery, they should ask about their interpretive experience, "What is *at stake* if visitors leave our site without an accurate, balanced, and sensitive understanding of slavery and its full role in our history?" Over the past three decades, historic sites and museums have started to do more to incorporate stories of slavery into their interpretation. Major institutions such as the Colonial Williamsburg Foundation and the National Trust for Historic Preservation have led the way in sharing the lives of enslaved people at their sites. However, even today, visiting many southern plantations, antebellum historic house museums, or northern sites with histories intersecting that of slavery will likely tell a different story.[2] Here the lives and even physical presence of the enslaved have all but vanished, and the broader political, economic, and social context of slavery is nowhere to be found. Much has been written about the shortcomings of the public history profession in this regard. As sociologist Stephen Small noted about plantation museums, "The majority of these sites deploy a series of tactics to symbolically denigrate, marginalize, or trivialize slavery and its legacies. Their representation and treatment of … antebellum slave cabins reveals these tactics in striking ways because these cabins, when compared with mansions are neglected, distorted, or simply left out of accounts."[3]

How Do We Proceed?

Our organization, the Tracing Center on Histories and Legacies of Slavery, is committed to helping historic sites and museums work through concerns surrounding the interpretation of slavery and to find opportunities to share this important history with visitors. In several years of offering workshops and advice to help historic sites and museums interpret the history of slavery, we have been struck by the lack of literature with concrete advice for sites working to rectify the field's shortcomings in this area. As a result, the Tracing Center decided to take a closer look at moving the conversation forward.

To gain a better understanding of the state of the field and how we could help museums—including directors, curators, educators, interpreters, boards of trustees, and volunteers—present compelling historical narratives, the Tracing Center conducted a series of surveys to explore the field's perceived needs and challenges in interpreting slavery. Respondents described facing challenges like these:

- "telling the story in a way that fulfills our mission"
- "getting people who are skittish about slavery and 'black museums' in the door"
- "lack of extant built environment"
- "multiple claimants to the 'truth' of the enslaved experience"
- "getting volunteers and staff to discuss slavery on public tours"
- "being sensitive about the issue without sugar-coating it"
- "difficult to keep African American interpreters"
- "white resistance"
- "fear of locals"
- "lack of broader context"
- "the board"[4]

Each of these concerns has merit, but they are not insurmountable challenges. As we explored the results with our colleagues and leaders in the field,[5] a pattern began to emerge. We organized the responses into six categories, which constitute a framework that can be applied by historic sites and museums to help structure the development of a comprehensive and conscientious interpretation of slavery: (1) comprehensive content; (2) race and identity awareness; (3) institutional investment; (4) community involvement; (5) visitor experiences and expectations; and (6) staff training.

Organization of the Book

This book is organized according to the six components of a comprehensive and conscientious interpretation of slavery as outlined in the sidebar on page xv, with at least one chapter devoted to each of the six components. Each chapter presents an integral piece of the puzzle, providing practical tips, based on theory and research, to help museums and historic sites develop a plan for interpreting slavery.

In chapter 1, "Comprehensive Content and Contested Historical Narratives," we review the breadth and depth of the history of slavery in the United States, and we discuss how a

The Six Components of a Comprehensive and Conscientious Interpretation of Slavery

- **Comprehensive Content:** Sound interpretation of slavery begins with historical research about the role of slavery that is both broad—about your site as well as the role slavery played in the broader history of your community, state, and the nation—and deep, using a well-rounded narrative informed by individual stories.
- **Race and Identity Awareness:** The racial identity of both staff and visitors plays a role in how interpretation is offered and received. As professionals, we must be aware of, and comfortable with, our own knowledge and feelings about race and slavery. We must also understand where our visitors are coming from in order to help them understand their own concerns surrounding race and identity when learning about slavery.
- **Institutional Investment:** All of an institution's core constituencies—board, management, staff, and volunteers—must be invested in and support the institution's interpretation of slavery. Board and management establish the mission and vision for the site, make strategic decisions regarding the allocation of resources, and set the tone for how the institution approaches the subject affectively. All staff, not just those directly involved in the interpretation of slavery, play a major role in determining how the interpretive plan is implemented and in its success.
- **Community Involvement:** The (re)interpretation of slavery provides opportunities to connect your institution with new community partners, including individuals and organizations that might relate to, and find value in, the stories and perspectives of traditionally marginalized voices. Partners from the community should be actively involved in your site, helping to shape narratives, attending events, providing funding, donating objects, contributing research and stories, and advocating for your site.
- **Visitor Experiences and Expectations:** We don't "do" this ourselves—our visitors are equal partners in interpretation. We need to know what kind of preconceptions visitors bring with them, what their expectations of the visit are, and how their actual experiences match up to their expectations. We can then use that information to help shape relevant and engaging experiences for our visitors.
- **Staff Training:** How staff members are trained is an integral part of an institution's commitment to interpreting slavery, and this should be given the utmost time and attention. Trainers and staff need to discuss the nuances of creating a content-balanced, affectively balanced narrative and how to help visitors scaffold their knowledge and fashion new historical narratives out of cognitive dissonance.

comprehensive interpretation of slavery will clash with traditional historical narratives at the heart of identity for many American visitors. The history of slavery in the United States is broader and deeper than our public memory generally acknowledges, encompassing all regions of the country, individuals from all walks of life, and a wide range of economic activities, from seafaring and family farming to industrialization. This means that far more historic sites have their own historical connections to slavery to interpret than have generally done so, and wherever slavery is interpreted, a comprehensive and conscientious interpretation requires that the institution of slavery be set in the context of its broad and deep role in our nation's history.

Interpreting slavery well also means exposing staff and visitors to new historical narratives in which slavery played a much broader role in the history of the nation than our traditional public memory implies. Dismantling old narratives and replacing them with new, and historically more accurate, alternatives may be healthy and productive. But this process can generate resistance, resentment, or outright disbelief, and it requires careful thought and sensitive handling for a successful outcome. Chapter 1 explores ways in which our traditional historical narratives make slavery a treacherous topic for interpretation and considers how to help both staff and visitors assimilate new information about the history of slavery. Among the techniques we recommend is the act of bringing the history of slavery to life through the power of individual stories, especially those that go beyond traditional slave narratives, to reflect the historical agency of free and enslaved black Americans—and here again, the broader context of slavery proves to be an essential starting point.

We turn to the second of our six components for interpreting slavery, that of race and identity awareness, in chapter 2, "The Role of Race and Racial Identity in Interpretation." For staff and visitors alike, the interpretation of slavery evokes powerful emotions and challenges narratives at the core of racial and other forms of identity. It's important that staff be given opportunities to explore their own racial barriers so that they can begin to understand their racial preconceptions, any gaps in their knowledge, and any emotions that are awakened when engaging this material before trying to engage with the public. Confronting this history and its living legacy raises a powerful stew of emotions. For staff to confront these sensitive issues requires more than a set of readings or listening to an experienced trainer speak—this process is about both "head" and "heart." In chapter 2, we provide some background about race and racial identity, and we ask what can be done about the ways in which issues of race interfere with the interpretation of slavery, so that staff can proceed in relative comfort to do their jobs well and so that visitors can experience the interpretation without undue discomfort or resistance.

Linnea Grim, director of education and visitor programs at Thomas Jefferson's Monticello, explores how four historic sites have navigated the bumpy road of institutional support in chapter 3, "'So Deeply Dyed in Our Fabric That it Cannot Be Washed Out': Developing Institutional Support for the Interpretation of Slavery." When boards and executive teams foster support for shifting from memorializing dominant white history to offering broader, more inclusive narratives, they make this new interpretation central to planning, secure funds and staffing for relevant initiatives, and create internal and external awareness. Obtaining such support can be especially challenging in the area of slavery, and an institution's staff must be fully committed to the interpretation from top to bottom, trustees to volunteers. Linnea offers lessons for obtaining institutional support on the basis of her case studies of Philipsburg Manor in New York State, and of George Mason's Gunston Hall, George Washington's Mount Vernon, and Monticello, all in Virginia.

Introducing or transforming the interpretation of slavery often poses a particular challenge at historic sites in the North, or elsewhere outside the South, in part because of the necessity of changing the institution's *culture*. Katherine Kane, executive director of the Harriet Beecher Stowe Center, explores this topic through a series of case studies in chapter 4, "Institutional Change at Northern Historic Sites: Telling Slavery's Story in the Land of Abolition." Organizational change can be complex and difficult, requiring reflection, interaction, and committed leadership, and there are many ways for historic sites to experience success or failure when seeking to significantly alter the interpretation they offer the public. To highlight the variety of approaches to institutional transformation in the context of interpreting slavery, Kane analyzes the different ways in which five northern historic sites have undertaken this task. Her case studies include four historic homes in the Northeast—Royall House and Slave Quarters, formerly a 500-acre slave plantation in Medford, Massachusetts; Linden Place, a mansion built by slave traders in Bristol, Rhode Island; Cliveden, a 1767 Philadelphia home belonging to one of the region's largest slave-owning families; the Harriet Beecher Stowe Center in Hartford, Connecticut—and the Mattatuck Museum in Waterbury, Connecticut, which found itself embroiled in controversy for displaying the skeleton of an enslaved resident of the town. Kane draws lessons for institutional transformation from each of these sites by asking what drove institutional change processes, who was involved, what barriers were encountered, what impact the changes had, and whether those changes have "stuck."

In chapter 5, "The Necessity of Community Involvement: Talking about Slavery in the Twenty-First Century," Dina Bailey, of the National Center for Civil and Human Rights in Atlanta, and Richard Cooper, of the National Underground Railroad Freedom Center in Cincinnati, address the pitfalls and opportunities inherent in involving the community in the (re)interpretation of slavery. A site's community can be broadly defined in terms of visitors, educators, scholars, donors, and other stakeholders who support, challenge, and retain an interest in the institution and its mission. Active community involvement makes institutions stronger and more relevant to the wider community and to potential visitors, deepens perspectives, and creates opportunities that have more significance and impact. Bailey and Cooper share their strategies for developing and implementing a community involvement plan to ensure a more relevant and successful institution.

Professional evaluator Conny Graft explores the subject of visitor experiences and expectations concerning the interpretation of slavery in chapter 6, "Visitors Are Ready, Are We?" An often expressed concern from museums is "Our visitors don't want to hear about slavery. They've come for an enjoyable experience; slavery will only upset or depress them." We believe that statements like these sell visitors short. Studies show that visitors want to learn both the good *and* the bad in our nation's history. More than that, visitors want to talk about this history with us and with each other. Graft breaks down extant visitor studies conducted by historic sites that interpret slavery, including the African Burial Ground National Monument in New York City and the Smithsonian National Museum of African American History and Culture. She analyzes these and other sources of data about visitor experiences and expectations, and she shares how knowing more about our visitors can help us create better experiences for them, with some tips for planning and implementing visitor evaluations at your own site.

The final component of a comprehensive and conscientious interpretation of slavery is that of staff training—an especially important topic. We draw lessons for staff training in chapters 1 and 2 and at other points throughout the book, but this subject is given its own treatment by Patricia Brooks, former manager of African American Initiatives at Colonial Williamsburg, in chapter 7, "Developing Competent and Confident Interpreters." Telling complicated and controversial stories requires achieving interpreter comfort with historical content, visitor interactions, and interpretative techniques, including a sound understanding of how visitors receive and process challenging historical information.[6] Brooks provides advice on developing and conducting a training program that offers staff opportunities to talk about their concerns and work through new techniques to deliver a comprehensive and conscientious interpretation of slavery.

In chapter 8, "Perceptions of Race and Identity and Their Impact on Slavery's Interpretation," interpreter Nicole Moore blends the subjects of race and identity with issues of staff training, examining the especially challenging issue of how staff and visitor perceptions, based on each other's race, can affect the interpretation of slavery. It's impossible to do a tour about slavery without issues of race arising. Race is still taboo in some areas of the country and many Americans are uncomfortable with the topic. Should the race of the interpreter matter when interpreting slavery? How does the race of the visitor sway our interpretation? Moore spoke to front-line interpreters who confront the intersection of race and slavery on a daily basis. She explores how we, as narrators of history, are perceived by our audience and how we perceive our audience, and how these perceptions influence the delivery and reception of narratives about slavery.

> That US slavery has both officially ended, yet continues in many complex forms—most notably institutionalized racism and the cultural denigration of blackness—makes its representation particularly burdensome in the Unites States. Slavery here is a ghost, both in the past and a living presence, and the problem of historical representation is how to represent that ghost, something that is and yet is not.[7]

Taken individually, these chapters provide theory and practical tips for assisting museums and historic sites with their interpretation of slavery. This book aims to move the field forward in its collective conversation about the interpretation of slavery, always acknowledging the criticism of the past and acting in the present to develop an inclusive interpretation of slavery. Presenting the history of slavery in a comprehensive and conscientious manner is difficult and requires diligence and compassion—for the history itself, for those telling the story, and for those hearing the stories—but this is a necessary part of our collective narrative about our past, present, and future.

Notes

1. Jose-Marie Griffiths and Donald King, "InterConnections: The IMLS National Study on the Use of Libraries, Museums and the Internet," *Institute for Museum and Library Services*, 2008. http://www.interconnectionsreport.org/reports/IMLSMusRpt20080312kjm.pdf.
2. Jennifer L. Eichstat and Stephen A. Small, *Representations of Slavery: Race and Ideology in Southern Plantation Museums* (Washington, D.C.: Smithsonian Books, 2002).
3. Stephen A. Small, "Multiple Methods in Research on 21st Century Plantation Museums and Slave Cabins in the South," in *Rethinking Race and Ethnicity Research Methods*, ed. John H. Stanfield II (Walnut Creek, Calif.: Left Coast, 2011), 185.

4. The Tracing Center on Histories and Legacies of Slavery, "Surveys of Historic Site Employees" (unpublished study, Watertown, Mass., 2012).
5. Colleagues who helped develop the Tracing Center's workshop on interpreting slavery and contributed to the formatting of the components of "Comprehensive and Conscientious Interpretation": Patricia Brooks, Conny Graft, and Julia Rose.
6. For instance, research suggests that listeners initially respond to information contradicting their worldview by ignoring information, counterarguing, or questioning the source of the information. These behaviors are to be expected and embraced, not treated as signs of failure. One example of a way to ease this process for visitors is to avoid telegraphing challenging historical information before presenting a suspenseful narrative. See Sonya Dal Cin, Mark Zanna, and Geoffrey T. Fong, "Narrative Persuasion and Overcoming Resistance," in *Resistance and Persuasion*, eds. Eric S. Knowles and Jay A. Linn (Mahwah, N.J.: Lawrence Erlbaum, 2004), 177–78. Compare Julia Rose, "Interpreting Difficult Knowledge," American Association for State and Local History, Technical Leaflet #255 (2011).
7. Michel-Rolph Trouillot, *Silencing the Past: Power and the Production of History* (Boston: Beacon, 1995), 146.

CHAPTER 1

Comprehensive Content and Contested Historical Narratives

KRISTIN L. GALLAS AND
JAMES DEWOLF PERRY

THE UNITED STATES suffers from a form of collective amnesia about much of our history of slavery, and especially about its breadth and depth throughout our society and across the country. The historical experience of slavery in the United States goes far beyond the traditional narrative of enslaved Africans picking cotton or cutting sugarcane on large southern plantations. As a result, far more museums and historic sites have a history of slavery to interpret than is commonly acknowledged, and far more Americans are connected to this history, through family, regional, or institutional ties, than suspect that they do.

A Portrait of Slavery in the United States

Consider the following historical narratives:

- On Valentine's Day 1783, an elderly free woman named Belinda successfully petitioned the Massachusetts General Court for a pension for a half-century of enslavement on a 500-acre plantation outside of Boston, now a historic site known as Royall House and Slave Quarters.[1]
- In 1803, two enslaved children, Adjua and Polydore, were purchased by James DeWolf on the West African coast and brought back to Bristol, Rhode Island, on his ship *Lavinia*, where they served the DeWolf family for the rest of their lives.[2]
- In 1844, Robin and Polly Holmes and their children were brought from Missouri to Oregon by their owner, Nathaniel Ford, and remained enslaved on his Willamette Valley farm.[3]

Figure 1.1. The weave room at Lowell National Historical Park's Boott Cotton Mills Museum in Lowell, Massachusetts still rings with the thumping of looms and the whirling of belts and pulleys as it maintains the tradition of producing cotton textiles.
Source: National Park Service/Jonathon Parker.

- Adelia Gates, a botanical illustrator whose collection at the Smithsonian Institution amounts to 600 works, got her start as a "Lowell girl" working in brutal conditions in one of the many cotton textile mills dotting the Northeast in the first half of the nineteenth century.[4]
- On December 15, 1860, Richard Lathers, a leading New York City merchant, organized a rally of 2,000 merchants, bankers, and shipping magnates on Wall Street to address the growing threat of Southern secession, declaring that their "sympathies have always been with Southern rights and against Northern aggression."[5]
- On May 12, 1862, Robert Smalls, the enslaved steersman of the Confederate steamer *Planter*, seized the ship and delivered it safely out of Charleston's harbor to the United States Navy, in what the *New York Herald* called "one of the most daring and heroic adventures since the war commenced."[6]

Together, these anecdotes hint at the full geographical extent and economic importance of US slavery and at the great diversity of experiences of slavery and the ways in which those who were enslaved engaged in active resistance against enslavement.

A comprehensive portrait of slavery in the United States would surely include scenes of enslaved people toiling on southern plantations. It would also include pictures of domestic servants, coachmen, and the like. But those enslaved in this country were also dockworkers

Figure 1.2. The Royall House (background) and slave quarters (foreground) were home to the largest slaveholding family in Massachusetts and to the enslaved Africans who made this lavish way of life possible.
Source: Theresa Kelliher/Royall House and Slave Quarters.

in Boston, New York, and Philadelphia; field hands on plantations in Connecticut and Massachusetts; blacksmiths in Rhode Island; and those who traveled to the Midwest and the West with their masters, where, among other occupations, many toiled on small family farms. There were full-fledged slave plantations in the Northeast—several of which are interpreted as such today, including Sylvester Manor, originally an 8,000-acre plantation on Long Island, and Royall House and Slave Quarters (figure 1.2), formerly a 500-acre plantation known as Ten Hills Farm outside of Boston.[7] Yet, most of those enslaved in the Northeast were not clustered on large agricultural plantations but distributed on small farms, in coastal cities, and across many households. In Connecticut, Massachusetts, and Rhode Island, for instance, as many as one in four white households included at least one enslaved person by the time of the American Revolution. In Connecticut at that time, it has been estimated that "half of all ministers, half of all lawyers and public officials, and a third of all doctors" owned at least one slave.[8]

White Americans are also an integral part of this comprehensive portrait of US slavery. Many white people lived and worked alongside enslaved blacks, while the rest were, in one way or another, enmeshed in economic systems based on complicity in slavery. The northeastern United States, for instance, sent out 85 percent of the nation's slaving voyages, and the infamous "triangle trade" and the colonial provisioning trade to slave plantations in the West Indies were important enough to the northern colonies that John Adams, second president of the United States, remarked, "I do not know why we should blush to confess that Molasses was an essential Ingredient in our Independence."[9] Slave-owning itself was far more widespread in the Northeast, Midwest, and West than the public generally suspects, lasted far longer than many recognize today, and was no less harsh in practice than slavery in the South. The primary economic impetus for the nation's westward expansion, prior to the Civil War, was the demand for foodstuffs produced for southern slave plantations. Finally, the national economic importance of southern, slave-produced cotton cannot be overemphasized. Cotton was the leading export of the United States from 1803 until the eve of World War II, amounting to 60 percent of all US exports at the outbreak of the Civil War. This economic activity enriched the South, certainly, but much of the vast profits from southern cotton production flowed north and west, especially to commercial centers such as New York, Boston, and Philadelphia. Cotton was also essential to the textile industry, which was at the heart of the Industrial Revolution, and slave-produced cotton fueled the textile mills in the Northeast and elsewhere that industrialized the United States.[10]

Slavery thus played an essential role in the history now interpreted at a multitude of historic sites throughout the nation, including historic homes, small family farms, commercial centers, industrial sites, and large-scale plantations. By interpreting this history, we can tell more comprehensive and balanced stories about our sites and about all who lived or worked there, including bringing out the voices of the marginalized. Just as importantly, we can expand visitors' understanding of the contributions of slavery—and of the lives of enslaved African Americans—to the political, economic, and social life of the entire nation. Finally, because slavery is a painful chapter in our nation's history, and one fraught with implications for our society today, there is tremendous value in helping visitors to understand that the institution of slavery wasn't merely the responsibility of the South or of a wealthy elite. It was a cornerstone of the nation's economy and society—and an engine of upward mobility for millions of American families.

Comprehensive Content

Comprehensive content starts with the recognition that the history of slavery in the United States is broader and deeper than our public memory generally acknowledges, and that far more sites have a historic connection to slavery to interpret than have generally done so. The brief portrait of slavery we have just offered might be used to inspire fresh research into the direct and indirect connections of any particular historic site to slavery. Comprehensive content also includes bringing the history of slavery to life through the power of individual stories, especially those that go beyond traditional slave narratives to reflect the historical agency of free and enslaved black Americans, and, here again, the broader context of slavery can be helpful. The stories of individuals who were enslaved can be brought to light with a conscious awareness of the full spectrum of circumstances within which the enslaved found themselves in this nation, including geography, time periods, and occupations. Historical agency, meanwhile, can best be conveyed with a full appreciation of the ways in which slavery was experienced and resisted.

One basic rule of thumb when interpreting slavery is that in the United States slavery was not a monolithic institution. Its stories are wide-ranging and multifaceted. Each individual's story of slavery was unique. These stories must be set in a proper context starting with the individuals, spiraling out to include the site, the neighboring community, the state, the region, and the country. As staff research the history of people enslaved on their site, they need to be aware that generalizations of the "slavery experience" are neither appropriate nor compassionate. Audiences expect to hear affective stories of individuals—black and white, enslaved and free—set into the context of the history of the site and the broad historical context of slavery.

To do this, historians and interpreters need to think inclusively about the narratives their visitors will experience. In shaping these narratives, do not just rely on the historical "facts." Weave them into a compelling (true!) story. No need to embellish the past; it's interesting enough without falsifying or generalizing. Look at your landscapes, structures, and objects in a different way. How can you use them to tell a more powerful story? Based on your research, what was day-to-day life like? How can you help visitors to imagine the life of your plantation during its peak years of slave labor? These strategies and more can help in preparing an interpretation that will bring your history to life, open up new interpretive opportunities, and be more relevant to your visitors.

Our distorted public memory of slavery contributes to making this a challenging history to interpret, as does the fact that this story involves the painful invocation of episodes of trauma, violence, and oppression.[11] We believe there are two issues that make the interpretation of slavery (and similarly controversial histories) especially challenging for museums and historic sites: the ways in which this history invokes *contested narratives* and how *racial identity* influences the experience of interpreters and visitors. We address these topics in this chapter and the rest of the next.

Historical Narratives and Identity

All people, including site staff and visitors, have identities that define how they see themselves, how they make sense of the world, and how they interact with others. Although identity is in part individual in nature and in part based on specific roles we play in the social world, we are speaking here of identities based on membership, actual or perceived, in social groups.[12] These collective or group identities may include national, regional, and local identities, identities based on family or workplace, and identities based on race or ethnicity, social class, and religion, among many others. People possess multiple identities at any given time, and the salience of these identities will vary depending on life experience, with whom the person is interacting at any given time, and their emotional investment in the meaning of each identity.[13]

These identities, in turn, are largely based on *narratives*. The use of narratives, and more traditional concepts such as myth and storytelling, to explain identity has long been the province of the humanities. Often, these were simple, even primordial tales, such as the flood myth that recurs in so many cultures.[14] Even specific historical episodes, such as the apocryphal tale of young George Washington and the cherry tree, were often short, simple stories with clear lessons. In recent decades, however, there has been an explosion of work in the social sciences on conceptualizing narratives as being at the core of identity:

> It is through narrativity that we come to know, understand, and make sense of the social world, and it is through narratives and narrativity that we constitute our social identities [and] come to be who we are.[15]

A portion of this emerging work on narrative and identity, especially in the field of psychology, has concentrated on the individual life-stories people construct for themselves.[16] In other fields, including sociology, history, and anthropology, however, the focus has been on shared, collective narratives.[17] Any given individual may have choices over which group narratives to internalize as part of their identity, but these narratives themselves are generally not held consciously and are "rarely of our own making."[18]

Collective narrative, or shared memory, "plays a major role in ... sustaining a sense of self in and through the communities in which individuals belong and relate to others."[19] This process is "not a remembering but a stipulating: that *this* is important, and this is the story about how it happened."[20] Indeed, the value of collective narratives is so great that they are "the key to understanding why people invest so much in retaining a certain identity."[21] Many of these collective narratives are about historical episodes, including grand historical narratives that are widely shared, on topics such as how the United States came to be, how families have prospered here, and about the nation's defining values.[22] "Historical narratives not only sustain shared memories, but also make 'a *social identity* explicit,'" by differentiating that identity from others.[23] In short, "our histories shape our identities."[24]

Historical narratives can be compiled directly from specific events, but they are also constructed from "schematic narrative templates." These templates dictate patterns into which stories should be shaped and provide the lessons or values that should arise out of each tale.[25] In the case of the United States, for instance, many national and subnational historical narratives are organized around such themes as independence, self-reliance, entrepreneurship, and the value of hard work and the American Dream. Think, for instance, of Horatio Alger's stories, which tended to follow a distinctive narrative pattern, complete with shared themes and outcomes reflecting classical American ideals. Just as people hold multiple identities, they can possess historical narratives simultaneously about their families, their regions, their racial or ethnic groups, their social classes, their workplaces, and their nation, among others.[26]

Narratives of Slavery and American Identity

In the United States, our limited public recollection of slavery contributes to historical accounts about the nation, its regions, its social classes, and its families and institutions in which slavery plays little or no part, aside from its role in the history of African Americans and of a few wealthy plantation-owning families in the South. This is true even for visitors who may appear, on the surface, to know little or nothing about slavery. Even though it may seem as if "visitors at today's sites no longer come with as much—or sometimes, with any—historical knowledge," especially on a topic like this, there are powerful, but often implicit, understandings about slavery, or its absence, lurking at the heart of many American identity narratives.[27]

In the Northeast, for instance, many (white) Americans have identities based on stories in which their families, their region of the country, their socioeconomic class, and the nation as a whole found success without depending much, if at all, on enslaved labor. Instead, their identities usually rely on stories emphasizing themes such as self-reliance, entrepreneurship, free labor, and individual merit.

To put this in terms of family identity, for convenience, this is true of those from the Northeast whose heritage stretches back to colonial times: their narratives may emphasize small-scale farming or commerce, but rarely with any hint of the ownership of enslaved people or of economic activity dependent upon slavery, the transatlantic slave trade, or commerce with slave plantations in the West Indies, all of which were critical to the economic success of settlers in the northern colonies. Those whose families immigrated to these shores after the founding of the United States may have slightly different narratives, invoking perhaps hard labor in one of the Northeast's many textile mills, or discrimination against Irish or Italian immigrants in one of the Northeast's great port cities. Here, too, the narrative is likely to emphasize beginning with very little and making progress through free labor, hard work, and perhaps an entrepreneurial spirit; rarely discussed are the enslaved Americans who picked the cotton supplying the textile mills or who lived and worked in those port cities.

Antebellum historical narratives of families from the Midwest and the West, especially in the "free states," similarly tend to omit the presence, and the critical economic role, of slavery in these regions. Instead, the collective memory of these parts of the nation often focuses on families moving westward to farm a small plot of land or engaging in commercial or other economic activity in frontier territories. The reasons why Americans were moving west in those days, and the economic activity in which those regions engaged, prior to the Civil War, are conveniently absent from these narratives.

Many of these family narratives do incorporate slavery but not in historically realistic ways. Northern families, for instance, often presume that their ancestors were abolitionists, despite the relative unpopularity of that cause prior to the Civil War. Likewise, far more northern homes feature tales of the Underground Railroad than can be supported by the facts. Most significantly, those whose ancestors lived in the North by the time of the Civil War almost invariably seem to have internalized a narrative in which their forebears sacrificed dearly for the cause of emancipation, merely by fighting for (or otherwise supporting) the Union during the war. The fact that the Union did not go to war to emancipate the South's slaves (whatever the reasons the Confederacy went to war), and the highly controversial nature of emancipation in the North until the waning days of the conflict, do not disturb these often passionate narratives about families paying dearly for the racial sins of others.

Other white families in this country trace their ancestry back to European immigrants who arrived here after the formal end of slavery in 1865. For these Americans, historical narratives tend to focus on the themes of immigration: arriving on these shores with little in the way of education or possessions, for instance, and having to work hard, often at low-paying jobs and in the face of discrimination, to provide better opportunities for children and grandchildren. In these cases, slavery is usually entirely absent from the narrative, and this often seems to be a point of pride when the subject of slavery arises at an historic site. These narratives have their own particular problems in relation to the history of race in this country—such as the fact that these immigrants, as low as their status may have been when they arrived at Ellis Island or elsewhere, were still afforded opportunities for advancement, for themselves and their children, largely denied to millions of existing (black) American families until the 1950s and beyond. Yet the history of these immigrant families is also entangled with the slavery of pre–Civil War days in ways which their narratives deny. For instance, white immigrants arriving after emancipation were afforded all of the advantages of a society that had prospered largely through the exploitation of slave labor. European immigrants also came here primarily because there was a demand for labor, and that demand existed in large part because of the crucial role played by slavery in the economic success, and especially the industrialization, of the antebellum United States.

Although we have been talking in terms of family identity, the elements of these historical narratives are by no means limited to identities based on family. Local communities and states throughout the nation, outside of the "slave states," tend to feature variations of these narratives, as appropriate for local history. The same is true of a wide variety of institutions, such as churches, schools, colleges and universities, and social groups, and of larger institutions, such as national religious denominations.[28]

In the South, where the memory of slavery is harder to escape, historical narratives tend to acknowledge the presence of slavery but also to make slavery irrelevant to identity for other reasons. Many white families from the South, for instance, have incorporated a historical narrative into their identity in which their ancestors were not wealthy plantation owners but were of more modest means. In this account, the implication is that the family didn't own slaves, somehow didn't benefit from the southern slave economy, and perhaps even are believed to have suffered from competition with enslaved labor. Those southern families who know that they were slave owners, finally, may believe in a historical narrative in which slavery was often a brutal institution but in which their family was an exception to the rule. In this narrative, a particular slave-owning family was kind toward their slaves, and in return their slaves felt as if they were members of the family. The narrative may even extend to examples of the loyalty of the enslaved, during slavery or in the aftermath of emancipation.

It is no coincidence, of course, that the nation's public memory leaves out the connections of most American families and institutions to slavery. Because our historical narratives form the core of our identities, we tend to prefer "tightly constructed," unambiguous narratives, and to select historical facts that promote a positive view of the groups (family, region, race or ethnicity, nation) with which we identify.[29] This is especially true of conflict-ridden or other "difficult pasts," when groups or societies are often driven to processes of selective memory and collective historical amnesia.[30]

It may be worth noting also that historical narratives are often very different for those whose primary identities are not white, or settler, or immigrant, or perhaps even part of mainstream, white institutions. Just as painful or difficult historical episodes may not fit with the historical narrative of a dominant group, these may be "pivotal moments in the identity formation of sub-national groups," such as, in the cases of slavery or civil rights, the social construction of African American group identity.[31] These historical accounts, of course, not only include the history of slavery and racial discrimination, but they often follow different narrative templates, and surface different values and lessons, than do the nation's dominant historical narratives.

In fact, a primary reason for bringing the history of oppressed peoples to light is that "the narratives of excluded voices reveal 'alternative values' since narratives 'articulate social realities not seen by those who live at ease in a world of privilege.'"[32] Nevertheless, we must remember that all visitors, including those from nondominant groups, may have internalized some or all of our nation's dominant historical narratives as a core part of their *own* identities. This fact, though it complicates the task of interpreting slavery, is quite natural, because people often "incorporate for their identities the dominant story of the culture."[33]

Contested Narratives

Interpreting slavery well means exposing staff and visitors to narratives in which slavery played a much broader role in the history of the nation than our traditional public memory implies. As a result, staff and visitors will find themselves contending with narratives that tell how slavery was an essential part of the successes of the northern colonies, and of the northeastern, midwestern, and western states, and therefore of many white families and institutions that do not see their histories as intertwined with those of slavery at all.

This situation sets up a sharp clash between old and new narratives, which, because of the role played by historical narratives in identity, can cut to the core of a person's sense of self. It is not hard to see why this process is likely to be difficult and accompanied by resistance; after all, "struggles over narrations are," at heart, "struggles over identity."[34] Collective historical narratives are also created and maintained by many individuals, across diverse social and political contexts, and they are "preserved through social and ideological practices such as commemoration rituals, school and military parades, and national monuments,"[35] all of which adds to the difficulty of challenging shared narratives. This difficulty is not merely conceptual but emotional, too, and the emotional meaning of a collective narrative will vary with each individual.[36]

The challenge of confronting dominant historical narratives is magnified for painful histories like those of slavery—many Americans are reluctant to "confront painful historical episodes," and this is especially true of "racial histories" such as slavery or the civil rights movement.[37] We mentioned earlier the tendency of all people and social groups to avoid telling stories that reflect poorly on those they identify with, and surely slavery falls into this category for white Americans, and, somewhat paradoxically, for all who identify as American, including those who are African American or otherwise nonwhite. Slavery in the Americas, however, is more than merely a story of exploitation by perpetrators of injustice; it is also a story of violence, cruelty, and trauma virtually unparalleled in human history. The theory that the descendants of the enslaved are afflicted by intergenerational trauma may be controversial, but scholars are much more willing to entertain the idea that it is precisely through "collective narratives [that] there can be genuinely collective traumas insofar as historical events cannot easily be integrated into coherent and constructive narratives."[38]

At heart, however, the challenge of confronting our society's dominant narratives of slavery doesn't arise out of the trauma inherent in the history. New narratives are "dangerous," that is, "disruptive to the status quo," to the extent that they subvert the simplified narratives at the heart of the dominant culture's understanding of group identities. The danger doesn't lie in particular kinds of historical memories, but in the fact of "remembering the past in new ways that are disruptive to taken-for-granted assumptions about a group's identity." This clash of old and new narratives is inherently disruptive and unsettling because individuals are forced to "establish new understandings of personal and collective identities."[39] "Any memory can become dangerous when it resists the prevailing historical narratives."[40]

Dismantling old narratives and replacing them with new, and historically more accurate, alternatives may be healthy and productive. But this process can generate resistance, resentment, or outright disbelief, and it requires careful thought and sensitive handling for a successful outcome. When people confront information that does not fit within the narratives that inform their identities, they tend to experience "serious mental confusion," "powerlessness, despair, victimization," and other cognitive and emotional difficulties.[41] The process of integrating a new historical narrative into one's identity, and reconciling it with core beliefs and values, is a gradual one, involving fits and starts, and is mostly an unconscious process.[42] It is therefore essential that an interpretive plan and staff training take this process and its manifestations into account, and that visitors be given plenty of opportunity to express their cognitive and emotional struggles as they absorb the interpretation.

The Learning Crisis

What does the learning crisis arising from a visitor's exposure to a new historical narrative look like? In general, this is a messy process. After all, "challenging people's self-concepts and worldviews is threatening because they often feel anxious, fearful, confused, angry, guilty and resentful."[43] The process is also inherently lengthy and does not always produce immediate, visible results, because rather than assimilating new information, piece by piece, learners are gradually building up an alternative historical narrative, which continues to conflict with the original narrative until the latter can be modified or discarded. We cannot expect that the learning crisis will be resolved quickly or that it will unfold in a linear fashion, or in precisely the same way for each individual. We must also expect that the learner will respond to new information from both "head" and "heart" when a learning crisis centered on conflicting narratives at the core of identity invokes both cognitive and emotional responses.

One very useful approach to thinking about the learning crisis was introduced into the museum world by Julia Rose, director of the West Baton Rouge Museum. Rose, drawing primarily on Freudian psychoanalytic approaches, has identified several stages in the engagement of museum staff and visitors with "difficult knowledge," such as that of slavery. These stages, which do not necessarily play out in a particular order, or in any linear manner, include:

- Reception—a willingness, especially initially, to receive new information
- Resistance—negative expressions in response to threatening information
- Repetition—the instinct to repeat information that can't be easily assimilated
- Reflection—an internal process of readjustment, often expressed through discussion
- Reconsideration—a willingness, later in the process, to express new views and conclusions[44]

Another approach, which can expand on this picture of the learning crisis for those facing challenges to deeply held narratives, draws on the concept of cognitive bias. Leon Festinger, a social psychologist, coined the term "cognitive dissonance" to describe situations in which a person receives new information that conflicts with a preexisting belief or opinion, thereby creating a cognitive dilemma. That cognitive dilemma generates psychological discomfort, and it will manifest in cognitive mechanisms, many of them entirely unconscious, to minimize or avoid the dissonance if the cognitive conflict can't be readily resolved.[45] The gravity of this cognitive crisis will vary depending on the context and the importance of the information or belief at issue. In the case of historical narratives at the heart of one's identity, however, the crisis is unlikely to be mild, and this fact raises the importance of incorporating an understanding of cognitive bias into the interpretive process.

What behaviors does a learner exhibit when experiencing cognitive bias as part of wrestling with a new narrative? Such a learner may simply ignore conflicting information, at least for a time. The learner may also actively reject conflicting information, often with no apparent reason or rationalization.[46] In the case of conflicting narratives, this may be true not merely of new information that directly conflicts with information central to their existing narrative, but of any new information that tends to undermine the broad historical accounts on which their identity depends, whether or not that information appears to be significant. In other words, the details of stories, and the general tone of historical narratives, matters.

Learners experiencing biased processing may also attempt to rationalize their existing narratives or to counterargue against the new information and stories they're hearing. They may attempt to justify their beliefs in irrational ways, such as by appealing to tradition ("that's the way the story's always been told in this country; why change it now?").[47] A learner's cognitive defense mechanisms may also include questioning or belittling the source, understood as the interpreter personally or the scholarship on which the interpreter is drawing.[48] Finally, a learner may engage in expressions of resistance that appear to delay the incorporation of the conflicting information, such as complaining about the unpleasantness or relative unimportance of the new narrative, making jokes or sarcastic remarks, or acting out physically by attending to other matters or leaving altogether.[49]

Cognitive bias, or "confirmatory information processing," is not a rational process, even though it is a cognitive process. Many of these behaviors are manifestly not rational, and there are other irrational elements to how learners cope with cognitive bias, which interpreters should strive to take into account. The learning environment, for instance, can dramatically affect the extent to which learners engage in cognitive bias rather than try to incorporate new knowledge and perspectives. In general, a soothing environment, in which learners are encouraged to focus calmly and constructively on disturbing new information, may be best for resolving the learning crisis. However, recent research has shown, counterintuitively, that a tidy learning environment actually encourages cognitive bias, but a disordered or untidy setting reduces bias.[50]

Our focus on conflicting historical narratives emphasizes that the cognitive and emotional difficulties experienced during the learning crisis are likely to be largely unconscious.[51] This, too, has implications for how interpretation should engage, and respond to, learners. For instance, however deliberately obstructionist some visitor responses—such as resistance or denial—may appear, the visitor may sincerely be struggling with the interpretation—unintentionally, and likely without conscious awareness.

In sum, learners are likely to exhibit a combination of the following behaviors as they proceed through the learning crisis brought on by conflicting historical narratives:

- Ignoring new information
- Actively rejecting the new narrative
- Rationalizing the old narrative
- Counterarguing against the new narrative
- Justifying irrationally, as by appealing to tradition
- Expressing discomfort or lack of interest
- Questioning or belittling the source of information
- Physically disengaging
- Reflecting internally, or through external questions or discussion
- Repeating questions, concerns, or the new information itself
- Expressing a belief, at least in part, in the new perspective

It's important to understand that none of these behaviors are necessarily signs that the learner is rejecting the interpretation being offered. Rather, the negative behaviors are understandable and, often, necessary responses to a profound learning crisis cutting to the core of a person's identity, and, taken together, they reflect that the learner has not simply shut out the interpretation, but is engaging in the lengthy and challenging process of reconciling new information by internalizing a changed historical narrative (with all that this process implies for their self-identity).

Strategies for Interpreting Conflicting Narratives

What strategies for overcoming the learning crisis are suggested by an understanding of the role of historical narratives, such as those involving slavery, in the identities of staff and visitors? This process is, first and foremost, about guiding learners, not forcing them, as they are exposed to narratives that conflict with their core identities. As education specialist Stephen Brookfield puts it:

> Trying to force people to analyze critically the assumptions under which they have been thinking and living is likely to serve no function other than intimidating them to the point where resistance builds up against this process. We can, however, try to awaken, prompt, nurture, and encourage this process without making people feel threatened or patronized.[52]

In keeping with what we know about conflicting historical narratives and cognitive processing, the interpretation of slavery should embrace contradiction, conflict, and emotional responses in the learning process. This is, after all, how such learning takes place. If we are to take seriously institutional mission statements and professional standards that call for the education of visitors, there are simply no conflict-free shortcuts to interpreting challenging history.

The first step in embracing the learning process is to avoid telegraphing the conflict between the new narrative and traditional narratives visitors are likely to maintain as part of their identities. Psychologists believe that resistance to new information increases when the learner is forewarned that the information they will be receiving is likely to clash with what they already believe, or that the information will be presented in an attempt to persuade them to come around to another point of view.[53] So be honest, but don't frame the interpretation from the outset as being challenging to visitor beliefs, or as an attempt to bring them around to another perspective. Let them figure this out for themselves as the interpretation unfolds.

How, then, can interpretation play out in healthy and constructive ways? The single most effective technique for interpreting challenging history is narrative storytelling. Storytelling helps to ease listeners into the learning process, allows them to begin absorbing new information naturally and gradually, and gives them time to figure out the broader implications of the stories at their own pace. Narrative as an interpretive device is also less likely to come across as a deliberate attempt at persuasion than rhetoric is, and if presented with sufficient suspense, storytelling also helps to avoid telegraphing the conflicting nature of the broader narrative being interpreted.[54] Storytelling has the further advantage that it emphasizes the institution's authority by illustrating any interpretive themes (implicit or explicit) through detailed, factual historical accounts that visitors find intuitively harder to question than abstract statements. Finally, storytelling is perhaps the best strategy for engaging visitors in a challenging learning process that comes across, at least initially, as reasonably entertaining.

The extent to which narrative storytelling is persuasive depends, in large part, on how much the listener becomes involved in their own learning process while being *transported* into the story. To that end, the listener should ideally be fully engaged in the story, cognitively and emotionally, through strong and compelling storytelling and through feelings of suspense and the use of vivid imagery.[55] Here is one situation in which the importance of *affective equality* can be seen: encourage the listener's empathy with all historical figures, including both slave owners and the enslaved, to keep them fully immersed in the storyline.[56] This approach will help to correct the tendency toward affective *inequality*, in which visitors are often encouraged to relate emotionally to privileged historical figures rather than to traditionally marginalized actors. By encouraging learners to relate to all figures in a story, regardless of the visitor's identity or how we feel about the roles of the various historical actors, the learner will be more fully drawn into the story and thus more capable of overcoming cognitive biases impeding them from accepting the transformed narrative.

It is also important not to frame the interpretation of slavery as offering a new narrative to replace what may be the learner's dominant narrative. Doing so merely telegraphs the persuasive intent and sets up the cognitive and emotional challenge of reconciling conflicting narratives in the starkest possible terms. Introducing the interpretation gradually, through narrative storytelling, is one effective way to avoid such a jolting presentation, of course. Another approach is to frame the interpretation as building on the traditional narrative by incorporating *all* American voices and experiences into a single, more comprehensive narrative, including traditional voices (with important modifications, of course) along with traditionally marginalized groups. To do this in the context of the story of slavery, emphasize the parts of the narrative that can remain the same; these aspects might include, for example, the role of hard work, free labor, and industrialization in American prosperity. These elements of the traditionally dominant American narrative can be reinforced in the interpretation of slavery, which will be reassuring to many visitors. To maintain historical accuracy and balance, these themes must simply be placed in an expanded context, introducing the role played by slavery in how many Americans were able to prosper through hard work, free labor, and industrialization. This broader perspective on the American story will, of course, be challenging enough to those who have internalized the traditional narrative.

New content added to the traditional narrative can often be portrayed as entirely consistent with the *broader themes* of the narrative. For instance, slavery, too, is a story of a struggle to survive and to prosper, of triumph against the odds, and a struggle for freedom and equal opportunity. These all-American themes can make the new narrative not only more palatable, but also make the story of the enslaved, and of other traditionally marginalized groups, a central part of the traditional American narrative.

Portraying slavery using these themes from the traditional American narrative also allows for the incorporation of uplifting stories, not just tales of suffering and trauma, into the interpretation of slavery in a natural and seamless way. These more positive themes, though not the entire story of slavery, tend to be more palatable for learners of all races and backgrounds, and they make for a healthier learning process. Turning back to the concept of schematic narrative templates, the portrayal of uplifting stories arising out of slavery (and the stories of free black Americans) will be most effective if inserted into the narrative templates most commonly used for this country's dominant stories. This means framing stories of survival, of resistance, and of freedom-seeking, for instance, in the narrative structure traditionally employed for stories of survival in the wilderness, resistance to British rule prior to and during the American Revolution, and resistance to segregation during the civil rights movement.[57]

It's important to note that stories of human suffering and trauma during slavery have their place in interpretation. These are compelling stories with ample human interest, in addition to being an integral part of a balanced and conscientious interpretation of slavery. Historical accounts of suffering are effective at disrupting entrenched historical narratives that reinforce division into different social groups ("us" and "them"), thereby encouraging empathy, the development of solidarity, and the acceptance of disruptive, unified narratives.[58] Our fears about the impact of these traumatic stories on learners, especially when racial divisions are involved, tend to be overstated. For instance, research suggests that teaching black and white children about historical racism has positive effects, bringing children together across racial lines, and that concerns about emotional distress tend not to be borne out. However, with material of this kind, having an opportunity for careful dialogue, in which feelings can be explicitly acknowledged and discussed, can help greatly in increasing understanding, easing racial prejudice, and promoting positive racial feelings.[59] In ethnographic fieldwork with Coeur d'Alene Indians in northern Idaho, one anthropologist found that historical narratives of trauma and injustice, transmitted across many generations, were positive in nature, offering individuals resilience and strength as part of their identities.[60]

There are other concrete steps that institutions can take to embrace the behaviors that visitors exhibit during the learning crisis. First, institutions must ensure plenty of opportunities for visitors to express their resistance to the new narrative they are being exposed to. This means that interpretation needs to accommodate the anticipated visitor complaints about discomfort with the unpleasant nature of slavery and their claims that the stories being related are false, or irrelevant, or unimportant to the visitor or to the nation's story. This also means accommodating and responding appropriately to the jokes or sarcastic remarks and expressions of disbelief, which visitors honestly struggling with conflicting narratives may offer up. The same is true of the physical responses visitors may engage in, including distracting themselves or simply walking away from the interpretation. Finally, the interpretive process should anticipate and embrace the repetition that learners in crisis are likely to engage in, in the form of repeating questions, their own statements, and those of the interpreter.[61] These are not necessarily rejections of the interpretation, or unhealthy responses, but are natural expressions of cognitive and psychological struggles with new information, especially in the form of conflicting narratives that touch on matters of identity.

Learners struggling with conflicting narratives also require opportunities to engage in a process of self-awareness, self-examination, and reflection in order to begin to resolve the internal cognitive tension inherent in the process.[62] As Julia Rose advises, historic sites and museums should provide opportunities for visitors to talk, to ask questions, and to express their reconsideration of the interpretation's validity.[63] Ideally, the interpretive process should be heavily participatory, with ample opportunities for visitors to engage in discussion and dialogue with the interpreter and with one another. We know that visitors crave such opportunities when grappling with challenging history as long as they are not forced into participating.[64] If properly done, with sufficient staff training in facilitated dialogue and techniques for questioning and responding to visitors, these opportunities will allow visitors to reflect, engage the interpreter, express their fears and concerns, be heard, and know that their concerns are seen as legitimate and are taken seriously. There are other specific techniques for encouraging visitor reflection and engagement, such as opportunities for visitors to add their own reflections to a comment box, on a wall, or in an electronic display system.

Another concrete step for the interpretive process is to provide for repetition. As we have seen, learners require repetition when confronting deeply challenging information and struggling with cognitive bias before they can begin to respond outwardly in conventionally positive ways.[65] Don't just mention a single, new narrative at one point during a tour. Instead, introduce that narrative early on, without expecting immediate, positive results from many visitors. Then aid those visitors by reinforcing the new narrative (repeating information often, in new language but with the same content) and by providing new information frequently (adding additional details or telling the stories of other individuals). These techniques, by repeating information and by coming at the history from multiple angles, can reinforce and support the natural tendency of learners in crisis to seek repetition as they struggle to assimilate new information and transform internal narratives.

There is one final strategy we offer for helping visitors to navigate the learning crisis brought on by conflicting narratives, and that is flexibility. No two visitors are alike: "what a visitor brings with him/her to the museum experience in the way of prior experience, knowledge, interest and social relationships profoundly influences what s/he actually does and thinks about within the museum."[66] How true this is, especially when invoking history profoundly entangled with the narratives at the core of our selves—a history so deeply enmeshed in questions of racial identity. Institutions must engage with learners, as part of providing instructional scaffolding, in order to understand what they know and what they believe, and to respond accordingly. Adjust interpretation to build on the existing knowledge of visitors, to spend time on what they need to know or to work through, and to engage with their particular concerns and sensitivities. Visitors may not know exactly where their discomfort with the material comes from or what historical narrative they hold that is being challenged by the interpretation. This is another area where good staff training plays a critical role in helping interpreters to recognize not only the signs of a learning crisis, but also the elements of the traditional historical narratives that are often challenged by a comprehensive and conscientious interpretation of slavery.

We have phrased the advice in this section in terms of the visitor, but this guidance applies equally well to front line interpretive personnel (and to other staff and key constituencies). Part of staff training is going through the learning process described in this chapter so that staff can work through their own internal issues with the historical subject of slavery and its implications today. Another part of staff training is studying about the learning process, and how to employ strategies like these for addressing that process, in order to be able to interpret slavery effectively for the public.

In summary, we offer the following advice:

1. Embrace contradiction, conflict, and emotional response in the learning process.
2. Encourage learners to confront contradictions between old and new narratives; provoke them, but don't force them.
3. Avoid telegraphing the conflict between traditional historical narratives and the new narrative being interpreted.
4. Introduce the interpretation gradually, through narrative storytelling, and draw learners in using affective equality.
5. Frame new historical narratives as variations on traditional narratives, emphasizing all-American themes common to both, such as struggles for survival, freedom, and equal opportunity.
6. Balance the suffering and trauma of slavery with uplifting stories of survival and resistance, using traditional narrative templates for maximum effect.
7. Use the suffering and trauma of slavery to disrupt traditional narratives, encouraging empathy, solidarity, and the acceptance of broader, more inclusive narratives.
8. Provide space—physical, emotional, and cognitive—for visitors to express resistance in the face of new narratives.
9. Allow visitors to engage in reflection and discussion as part of their learning process through skilled questioning and facilitated dialogue.
10. Repeat information throughout the interpretive experience, and provide multiple entry points—different perspectives and individual stories—to reinforce basic information and themes.
11. Meet each visitor where they are, recognizing their unique perspective, their own internal narratives, and the role of their particular racial identity and preconceptions.

Notes

1. C. S. Manegold, *Ten Hills Farm: The Forgotten History of Slavery in the North* (Princeton, N.J.: Princeton University Press, 2010), 228–36.
2. George Howe, *Mount Hope: A New England Chronicle* (New York: Viking, 1959), 127–28.
3. R. Gregory Nokes, *Breaking Chains: Slavery on Trial in the Oregon Territory* (Corvallis: Oregon State University Press, 2013).
4. Nora Lockshin, "Adelia Gates—Flower Painter or Botanical Illustrator," Smithsonian Institution Archives. http://siarchives.si.edu/blog/adelia-gates-flower-painter-or-botanical-illustrator.
5. Richard Lathers, *Biographical Sketch of Colonel Richard Lathers* (Philadelphia: J. B. Lippincott, 1902).
6. "NOAA identifies probable location of iconic Civil War-era steamer; former slave piloted Planter to freedom," National Oceanic and Atmospheric Administration, May 13, 2014. http://www.noaanews.noaa.gov/stories2014/20140513_civilwarshipwreck.html.
7. For more about Sylvester Manor, see Mac Griswold, *The Manor: Three Centuries at a Slave Plantation on Long Island* (New York: Farrar, Straus and Giroux, 2013). For Royall House and Slave Quarters, see Alexandra Chan, *Slavery in the Age of Reason: Archaeology at a New England Farm* (Knoxville: University of Tennessee Press, 2007); Manegold, *Ten Hills Farm*.
8. Joanne Pope Melish, *Disowning Slavery: Gradual Emancipation and "Race" in New England, 1780–1860* (Ithaca, N.Y.: Cornell University Press, 1998), 16–17.
9. John Adams to William Tudor, *The Works of John Adams, Second President of the United States with A Life of the Author, Notes, and Illustrations*, ed. Charles Francis Adams (Boston: Little, Brown, 1856), Correspondence 345, John Adams, letter to Judge William Tudor, August 11, 1818.
10. See, for instance, Gene Dattel, *Cotton and Race in the Making of America: The Human Costs of Economic Power* (Chicago: Ivan R. Dee, 2009).
11. See Julia Rose, "Three Building Blocks for Developing Ethnical Representations of Difficult Histories," American Association for State and Local History, Technical Leaflet #264 (2013).
12. Identity may be divided into four components: an individual identity unique to one person, a role-based identity (based on relationships and position within society), perceived membership in various social categories (such as being Christian or American), and actual membership in different social groups (such as a church or neighborhood). See Timothy J. Owens, Dawn T. Robinson, and Lynn Smith-Lovin, "Three Faces of Identity," *Annual Review of Sociology* 36 (2010):479–80. For our purposes, it is the latter two components of identity that are relevant.
13. For the concept of multiple identities with varying salience, see Stryker, *Identity Theory*, 482. On the nature of national identity, see Rodney Bruce Hall, *National Collective Identity: Social Constructs and International Systems* (New York: Columbia University Press, 1999).
14. The most popular exposition of this approach to narrative can be found in Joseph Campbell, *The Power of Myth*, with Bill Moyers, ed. Betty Sue Flowers (New York: Anchor, 1988).
15. Margaret R. Somers, "The Narrative Constitution of Identity: A Relational and Network Approach," *Theory and Society* 23 (1994):606. See also Elizabeth Birr Moje and Allan Luke, "Literacy and Identity: Examining the Metaphors in History and Contemporary Research," *Reading Research Quarterly* 44:4 (2009):427; Anna Sfard and Anna Prusak, "Telling Identities: In Search of an Analytic Tool for Investigating Learning as a Culturally Shaped Activity," *Educational Researcher* 34:4 (2005).

16. See, for instance, Dan McAdams and Kate C. McLean, "Narrative Identity," *Current Directions in Psychological Science* 22 (June 2013):233–38.
17. James V. Wertsch, "The Narrative Organization of Collective Memory," *Ethos* 36:1 (2008): 120; Zvi Bekerman and Michalinos Zembylas, *Teaching Contested Narratives: Identity, Memory and Reconciliation in Peace Education and Beyond* (Cambridge: Cambridge University Press, 2012), 54.
18. Somers, "Narrative Constitution of Identity," 606.
19. Bekerman and Zembylas, *Teaching Contested Narratives*, 55.
20. Ibid., 125–26, quoting Susan Sontag, *Regarding the Pain of Others* (New York: Farrar, Straus, and Giroux, 2003), 76–77.
21. Bekerman and Zembylas, *Teaching Contested Narratives*, 55. See also Milton Takei, "Collective Memory as the Key to National and Ethnic Identity: The Case of Cambodia," *Nationalism & Ethnic Politics* 4:3 (1998):59–78.
22. Abbas Barzegar, "The Persistence of Heresy: Paul of Tarsus, Ibn Saba', and Historical Narrative in Sunni Identity Formation," *Numen* 58 (2011):209, 212; Heinrich Best, "History Matters: Dimensions and Determinants of National Identities Among European Populations and Elites," *Europe-Asia Studies* 61:6 (2009); Alexander M. Danzer, "Battlefields of Ethnic Symbols: Public Space and Post-Soviet Identity Formation from a Minority Perspective," *Europe-Asia Studies* 61:9 (2009):1559.
23. Min-Dong Paul Lee, "Contested Narratives: Reclaiming National Identity through Historical Reappropriation among Korean Minorities in China," *Stanford Journal of East Asian Affairs* 5:1 (2005):101, citing, in part, Michel de Certeau, *The Writing of History* (New York: Columbia University Press, 1988), 45.
24. Elazar Barkan, *The Guilt of Nations: Restitution and Negotiating Historical Injustices* (New York: W. W. Norton, 2000), x, cited in Bekerman and Zembylas, *Teaching Contested Narratives*, 55. See also Lee, "Contested Narratives," 101 ("the main channel through which national identity is actively contended and negotiated is through historical narratives"), and Robyn Autry, "The Political Economy of Memory: The Challenges of Representing National Conflict at 'Identity-Driven' Museums," *Theory & Society* 42:1 (2013), 59 (discussing the role of historical narratives in the construction of subnational identities).
25. Wertsch, "Narrative Organization of Collective Memory," 122–24.
26. Jens Rydgren, "The Power of the Past: A Contribution to a Cognitive Sociology of Ethnic Conflict," *Sociological Theory* 25:3 (2007):226–27; Alistair Ross, "Multiple Identities and Education for Active Citizenship," *British Journal of Educational Studies* 55:3 (2007):287; Somers, "Narrative Constitution of Identity," 619.
27. Catherine M. Cameron and John B. Gatewood, "Seeking Numinous Experiences in the Unremembered Past," *Ethnology* 42 (Winter 2003): 55.
28. For a recent exposition of the historic connections of many US colleges and universities to slavery, despite their institutional narratives, see Craig Steven Wilder, *Ebony & Ivy: Race, Slavery, and the Troubled History of America's Universities* (New York: Bloomsbury, 2013).
29. Rydgren, "Power of the Past," 233.
30. Autry, "Political Economy of Memory."
31. Ibid., 57; Ron Eyerman, "Cultural Trauma: Slavery and the Formation of African American Identity," in Jeffrey C. Alexander, Ron Eyerman, Bernhard Giesen, Neil J. Smelser, and Piotr Sztompka, eds., *Cultural Trauma and Collective Identity* (Berkeley: University of California Press, 2004), 60–111.

32. Somers, "Narrative Constitution of Identity," 631, quoting Martha Minow, "Forward: Justice Engendered," *Harvard Law Review* 101 (November 1987):10.
33. Donald E. Polkinghorne, "Explorations of Narrative Identity," *Psychological Inquiry* 7:4 (1996):366.
34. Somers, "Narrative Constitution of Identity," 631.
35. Bekerman and Zembylas, *Teaching Contested Narratives*, 55–56.
36. Ibid., 129.
37. Autry, "Political Economy of Memory," 58.
38. Jeffrey K. Olick, "Collective Memory: The Two Cultures," *Sociological Theory* 17:3 (1999): 344. Olick is otherwise skeptical of psychoanalytic claims that individuals, much less groups, can be diagnosed with trauma from historical events. For two very different approaches supporting the intergenerational transmission of trauma, see Aaron R. Denham, "Rethinking Historical Trauma: Narratives of Resilience," *Transcultural Psychiatry* 45:3 (2008):391–414; Joy Degruy Leary, *Post Traumatic Slave Syndrome: America's Legacy of Enduring Injury and Healing* (Milwaukie, Oregon: Uptone, 2005).
39. Zembylas and Bekerman, *Teaching Contested Narratives*, 126–27.
40. Ibid., 130.
41. Somers, "Narrative Constitution of Identity," 617, 630. See also Sonya Dal Cin, Mark Zanna, and Geoffrey T. Fong, "Narrative Persuasion and Overcoming Resistance," in *Resistance and Persuasion*, eds. Eric S. Knowles and Jay A. Linn (Mahwah, N.J.: Lawrence Erlbaum Associates, 2004).
42. Rydgren, "Power of the Past," 232.
43. Diane J. Goodman, *Promoting Diversity and Social Justice: Educating People from Privileged Groups* (Thousand Oaks, Calif.: Sage, 2001), 38–39.
44. Julia Anne Rose, "Rethinking Representations of Slave Life at Historical Plantation Museums: Towards a Commemorative Museum Pedagogy" (Ph.D. diss., Louisiana State University, 2006); Julia Rose, "Interpreting Difficult Knowledge," American Association for State and Local History, Technical Leaflet #255 (2011).
45. Leon Festinger, *A Theory of Cognitive Dissonance* (Stanford, Calif.: Stanford University Press, 1957), 3–5.
46. Dal Cin, Zanna, and Fong, "Narrative Persuasion and Overcoming Resistance," 177.
47. See John M. Grohol, "Fighting Cognitive Dissonance & The Lies We Tell Ourselves," *World of Psychology*, October 2008. http://psychcentral.com/blog/archives/2008/10/19/fighting-cognitive-dissonance-the-lies-we-tell-ourselves/.
48. Dal Cin, Zanna, and Fong, "Narrative Persuasion and Overcoming Resistance," 177.
49. Rose, "Interpreting Difficult Knowledge," 4–5.
50. Julia Niedernhuber, Andreas Kastenmueller, and Peter Fischer, "Chaos and Decision Making: Contextual Disorder Reduces Confirmatory Information Processing," *Basic and Applied Social Psychology* 36:3 (2014):199–208.
51. Rydgren, "Power of the Past," 232.
52. Stephen D. Brookfield, *Developing Critical Tinkers: Challenging Adults to Explore Alternative Ways of Thinking and Acting* (San Francisco: Jossey-Bass, 1987), 11.
53. Richard E. Petty and John T. Cacioppo, *Communication and Persuasion: Central and Peripheral Routes to Attitude Change* (New York: Springer-Verlag, 1986).
54. Dal Cin, Zanna, and Fong, "Narrative Persuasion and Overcoming Resistance," 177–78.
55. Ibid., 181–82.

56. E. Arnold Modlin Jr., Derek H. Alderman, and Glenn W. Gentry, "Tour Guides as Creators of Empathy: The Role of Affective Inequality in Marginalizing the Enslaved at Plantation House Museums," *Tourist Studies* 11:3 (2011), 3–19.
57. Wertsch, "Narrative Organization of Collective Memory," 122–24.
58. Bekerman and Zembylas, *Teaching Contested Narratives,* 127, 131.
59. Julie M. Hughes, Rebecca S. Bigler, and Sheri R. Levy, "Consequences of Learning about Historical Racism among European American and African American Children," *Child Development* 78:6 (2007):1689–1705.
60. Aaron R. Denham, "Rethinking Historical Trauma: Narratives of Resilience," *Transcultural Psychiatry* 45:3 (2008):391–414.
61. These are strategies that arise out of work in psychology on cognitive processing and from the "Resistance" and "Repetition" stages of Julia Rose's "Commemorative Museum Pedagogy" for engaging learners with difficult knowledge. See Rose, "Interpreting Difficult Knowledge," 4–5.
62. Grohol, "Fighting Cognitive Dissonance."
63. Rose, "Interpreting Difficult Knowledge," 5–7.
64. Susie Wilkening, "Difficult Issues in History Museums," *Finding Community* (blog), December 9, 2013. http://findingcommunityengagingaudiences.blogspot.com/.
65. This is, in particular, the "Repetition" stage of Julia Rose's "Commemorative Museum Pedagogy." See Rose, "Interpreting Difficult Knowledge," 5.
66. John Falk, "Reconceptualizing the Museum Visitor Experience: Who Visits, Why and to What Affect?" November 6, 2011, 2. http://www.scribd.com/doc/169153304/Reconceptualizing-the-Museum-Visitor-Experience-Director-John-Falk.

CHAPTER 2

The Role of Race and Racial Identity in Interpretation

KRISTIN L. GALLAS AND
JAMES DEWOLF PERRY

THE HISTORY of slavery in the United States is not merely a painful part of our shared past, evoking trauma, violence, and oppression. Slavery is also a living history that conjures powerful emotions for many Americans because it raises issues such as racial justice, healing, and repair. A site's interpretive plan, and its training for staff and docents, must therefore take into account the cognitive and psychological challenges for staff and visitors alike as they confront this history.

Nicole Moore, in chapter 8, discusses how interpreters and visitors respond to each other's race and how this dynamic affects the interpretation of slavery. This chapter has a broader focus in that we survey the various ways in which race, and racial identity, affect how interpreters and visitors think and feel about the history of slavery, and how they engage with the subject. Moore's chapter provides valuable guidance for interpreters seeking to navigate how their race affects visitor responses to their interpretation, and vice versa, but this chapter offers information and advice for institutions and interpreters engaged in the process of preparing, intellectually and emotionally, to interpret slavery while navigating the variety of racial dynamics that are likely to arise in their interactions with visitors.

Understanding Issues of Race and Racism

In the twenty-first century, open expressions of racism have become far less common in the United States. More subtle manifestations of racial prejudice and privilege, however, continue to vex our society, and they are often operating beneath the surface during the interpretation of slavery. Sociologists and other scholars conceptualize the issue of race and

Figure 2.1. An interpreter talks with guests during the program "Workin' the Soil, Healin' the Soul," in which they visit an eighteenth-century rural kitchen, slave quarters, and agriculture and livestock fields of Great Hopes Plantation in Williamsburg, Virginia, for a look at day-to-day living of rural enslaved families.
Source: Colonial Williamsburg Foundation.

racial prejudice in a variety of ways. We use the categories discussed below for addressing key issues involved in understanding race and racism in the United States today, because we believe this structure highlights critical issues that most Americans face when discussing issues of addressing race with others.[1]

Overt Racism

Racial prejudice openly expressed through words and behavior is almost always intentional, and in a society where overt racism is viewed with hostility by many people, it generally occurs only among like-minded people. Those who would, for instance, express racism openly in front of strangers at an historic site or museum today are relatively few.

Although there are many white Americans who are still openly and intentionally racist, their numbers have diminished dramatically in recent decades. The challenge in discussing slavery and race today is that many white people have come to believe that this is the sole definition of racism. Such people don't consider themselves to be personally implicated in racial prejudice, and they may even believe, contrary to what research shows, that our society is now "color-blind" or "post-racial." They may therefore engage in more subtle forms of racial bias in conversation without hesitation or self-reflection. These comparatively minor acts of prejudice, often unconscious, are often referred to as racial "microaggressions." They may also simply "check out" of conversations about slavery and race that they believe are blaming white people for the history and legacy of race in the United States.

Unconscious Racial Bias

Unlike overt racism, unconscious racial bias remains pervasive at all levels of US society. Unconscious racial bias refers to the residual biases and stereotypes that many still hold about other racial groups because of our socialization and conditioning, despite our desire *not* to be prejudiced. Because this racial prejudice is unconscious, many Americans actually believe that they are free of any racial prejudice.

Unconscious racial prejudice can be demonstrated through the use of subtle psychological tests, designed to reveal powerful but hidden associations that people may have between, for instance, black people and crime. In "rapid priming," subjects might be asked to judge the behavior of an ambiguously threatening figure whose race is not specified. Whether test subjects interpret the figure as threatening tends to depend on whether they were "primed" before the question with an image of a black or white face flashed too quickly to be perceived consciously. Similarly, in a test of "implicit association," subjects are asked to quickly associate pairs of words, such as "white" and "black," with pairs related to stereotypes, such as "good" and "bad." Implicit association tests show that many people are able to associate concepts that match stereotypes, such as "white" and "good," more quickly than they are able to pair words that run contrary to stereotypes, such as "black" and "good." Taken together, these tests have "shown that deep negative associations form a hidden level of preferences in the minds of many persons directed against stigmatized racial groups."[2]

Implicit association tests have demonstrated that most white Americans exhibit split-second associations that evidence a pro-white and anti-black bias. Even black participants often display a pro-white bias on these tests.[3] The latter is an example of what is called "internalized oppression," a phenomenon in which people of color have internalized society's negative attitudes toward themselves and their racial or ethnic group. Internalized oppression illustrates how Americans of all racial and ethnic backgrounds may believe, to one degree or another, in the same racial stereotypes and distorted historical narratives that are usually associated with prejudiced white people.

It isn't hard to understand how the interpretation of slavery can be profoundly affected by unconscious racial stereotypes lurking in the minds of staff and visitors. Consider, for instance, the often observed problem in which some visitors arrive believing in such historical stereotypes as that of the lazy slave. This problem looks rather different in light of recent scholarship that helps us to understand how, for modern visitors of all races, there can be deeply held, if often unconscious, associations between African Americans and laziness, even today.[4]

Historical Myths

In order to understand many common racial attitudes in our society, we have to understand the nature of our country's prevalent historical myths. Many of us are conditioned to believe misleading historical narratives, which suggest that most white families, and our nation's communities and institutions, were not connected historically to slavery and racism. These historical myths have several damaging consequences. They can cause many Americans to believe, sincerely, that African American history has no broader implications for mainstream, white history or for the state of our country today. Black staff and visitors themselves can often be swept up in these historical myths, but others may be aware of alternate perspectives, which can lead to profound disconnects during discussions of slavery and race among white and black interpreters and visitors. These historical narratives about slavery are discussed more fully in chapter 1.

There are also damaging American myths and narratives that, while related to the traditional narratives discussed in the previous chapter, focus on more recent historical events. These historical accounts tend to focus on explaining how white people in this country arrived where they are independently, all the while dismissing today's racial inequalities as based on recent events that have little or nothing to do with slavery or discrimination. For instance, we are often told that anyone can succeed in this country, merely by pulling themselves up by their own bootstraps. We don't necessarily realize how much the achievement of the "American Dream" has depended on the head start given historically to white families, not just during slavery, but during the Jim Crow century that followed. The Jim Crow era is well-known for being a time when black families continued to be held back through discriminatory laws and practices, in education, and employment. Less well-known are the variety of federal programs benefiting white people, especially during the first half of the twentieth century, that provided large-scale governmental assistance to the public in areas such as homeownership, college education, and support for small businesses. These federal aid programs, amounting to a form of "white affirmative action," played a major role in building the nation's white middle class and in allowing immigrants from Europe to prosper and assimilate. Yet black families were largely excluded from these programs.[5]

Historical information such as this paints a very different picture than the conventional historical narrative of white families achieving success largely on their own and primarily through hard work. Understanding this history can help in explaining why the establishment of political and civil rights for black Americans in the 1950s and 1960s was not enough to level the playing field, and it can aid in debunking many popular myths that seek to explain enduring racial inequality in other ways, such as by focusing on the impact of welfare, the rise of single motherhood, or supposed deficiencies within black communities. Being able to debunk history and contemporary myths like these can go a long way toward enabling interpreters to respond to many of the skeptical comments and questions often raised by visitors confronting unsettling information about the history and legacy of slavery.

Institutional and Structural Racism

As we have just seen, our nation's historical myths regarding slavery and race contribute to erroneous popular explanations for contemporary racial inequality. These myths exist in part because they conveniently obscure an especially painful truth about the nation's history of racism, namely, that racial discrimination has given white people (and not just wealthy white people) systematic advantages over black people that endure to this day.

Two terms are relevant here. The first is "institutional racism," which refers to the ways in which organizations can collectively disadvantage people of color through their policies and practices. These institutional policies and practices may result from individual prejudice; more often, they are well-intentioned and, on the surface, color-blind and racially neutral.

Their impact, however, is anything but neutral, as the implementation of these policies and practices can perpetuate a distribution of outcomes that has its origin in much earlier times. "Structural racism" is a broader term, encompassing institutional practices as well as the historical and cultural context, and racial stereotypes and beliefs, which maintain racial advantages and disadvantages in our society. Assume, for example, that in one generation, white students are disproportionately represented at elite universities and in powerful institutions in society. Then in the next generation, even without racial prejudice, white students may benefit from having parents with elite educational backgrounds and greater access to influential networking opportunities. Even without there being any racial prejudice involved, the net result of institutional and structural racism is racial inequality in educational achievement, health and health care, employment, wealth, housing, and other life outcomes.

White Privilege

White Americans, taken as a whole, possess privileges they have not earned and, in most cases, have never asked for. Law-abiding white people have little to worry about when being followed in stores or pulled over by law enforcement, for example, nor are they judged by their skin color in most settings. Nor do white people suffer from institutional racism; on the contrary, they often benefit from advantages like those of social networks for institutional access, whether at elite levels or in less privileged circles, which perpetuates privileges for groups traditionally having had access to those networks.

Many of these examples of privilege are based on the absence of disadvantage, or on relatively subtle forms of advantage such as the ability to reach out to networks for assistance. Privilege is also an area in which most people tend to focus on the advantages they don't have, rather than the ones they do. Because any white person will be less privileged than at least some other white people, it is possible for many white people to be convinced that they are not among those privileged by race. For these reasons, privilege is frequently invisible to the privileged and can be a highly contentious topic.

Racial Baggage

"Racial baggage" refers to the psychological stew of emotions that so many of us bring to conversations about slavery, race, and racism. White Americans, African Americans, and other people of color can bring a wide range of emotions to the table: fear, guilt, resentment, anger, defensiveness, anxiety, nervousness, numbness, despair, grief, distrust, and even exhaustion. These emotions tend to be stirred up by conversations touching on race, even historically, and especially by conscientious interpretations of slavery seeking to paint an accurate, balanced history. Often an emotion expressed by a member of one group can trigger an opposing emotion in a member of another group, causing a vicious cycle (such as black anger and white defensiveness). It is hard to address painful history, or its implications for race and privilege today, in a calm, rational way without dealing with the unconscious biases and racial baggage that keep so many of us divided from one another. A site's interpretive plan must therefore take into account the cognitive and psychological challenges for staff and visitors alike as they encounter and discuss the history of slavery.

Navigating Racial Dynamics in Interpreting Slavery

Slavery is ground zero of race relations.

—*James and Lois Horton*[6]

What can an awareness of, and sensitivity to, racial dynamics and emotions tell us about how to interpret slavery and engage visitors in discussions about this history?

Feelings of Power and Feelings of Vulnerability

Katrina Browne, a descendant of the DeWolf slave traders of Rhode Island and producer/director of the PBS documentary about the DeWolf family's legacy, *Traces of the Trade: A Story from the Deep North*, has written about racial dynamics and their role in teaching and learning about slavery.[7] She divides the emotional consequences of confronting this history into *feelings of power and strength* and *feelings of vulnerability*, and she notes that although white people may often benefit from the power dynamics involved in discussing race, it is their feelings of vulnerability in these discussions that often interfere with healthy, productive, safe learning.[8] As educator Diane Goodman notes, "Few people from dominant groups feel powerful or greatly advantaged. Even though they are the so-called beneficiaries of oppression, they may feel victimized as well."[9]

The feelings of vulnerability that frequently come up for white people in these situations include, most notably, those of guilt and shame.[10] Browne identifies other such feelings, including defensiveness, nervousness, and a variety of fears: fear of being called racist, fear of black anger or judgment, fear of loss of group pride, and even fear of reparations or revenge for a history of slavery and racial oppression. The discomfort many white people feel in thinking about slavery and racism can also lead them to express hostility toward black people, including black interpreters, out of a misplaced desire to avoid these negative emotions. These feelings, Browne says, may be "risky" to talk about, because it may seem as if the focus is being put on the feelings of white people, but these vulnerable feelings are important, as they can lead to such effects as dissociation from the learning process and a lack of empathy for the historical figures being interpreted.[11] On the other hand, Tema Jon Okun has observed that guilt and shame can play a constructive role in learning and personal transformation.[12] There will also be white people who claim not to have any strong feelings about race at all. This, too, can be seen as a privilege of being white, but it is one that often seems to break down when these white people are confronted with the realities of slavery and its full extent in US history.[13]

Black people can experience comparable feelings of vulnerability during discussions about slavery and race. In fact, learning about slavery can be traumatic for many black Americans and may generate acute feelings, such as shame or distress. And it has been argued that the African American experience since slavery has often preserved and heightened awareness of the experience of enslavement, so that today, for many African Americans, "the psychological trauma seems to be still there as if slavery happened yesterday."[14] Perhaps worst of all, when it comes to learning about slavery, many black Americans recall the experience as painful and as inadvertently reinforcing messages of inferiority and humiliation.[15] On the other hand, if the interpretation is good, learning about slavery can also inspire "deep pride and dignity," even as the story of slavery itself can be seen as "one of the greatest survival stories ever."[16]

Lessons for Interpreting Slavery

We have suggested that the interpretation of slavery evokes powerful emotions, raises troubling and controversial issues such as unconscious bias and white privilege, and challenges narratives at the core of identity, for staff and visitors alike. What can an organization do about this so that staff can proceed in relative comfort to do their jobs well and so that visitors can experience interpretation without undue discomfort or resistance?

Our society's racial dynamics, and the emotions raised by the topics of slavery and race, are powerful enough that we must not neglect our interpretive staff. Those involved in interpretation, especially on the front lines with visitors, deserve careful training and the opportunity to engage in facilitated dialogue or other means of exploring and working through their thoughts and feelings on these topics. To do anything less would be to expose staff to raw emotions that would harm them and interfere with their work and thus leave them ill-prepared to engage in healthy and constructive discussions with visitors.

It's important that staff be given opportunities to explore their own emotional baggage so that they can understand their preconceptions, any gaps in their knowledge, and any emotions that this material stirs up, before trying to engage with the public. For staff to confront these sensitive issues requires more than a set of readings or listening to an experienced trainer talk. This process is about both "head" and "heart." The Tracing Center starts by helping an institution's staff confront historic myths about slavery and, especially, about the role played by slavery in the history of all families in this country. Because this history clashes with widely held narratives, the learning process can generate significant cognitive dissonance. At the same time, confronting this history and its living legacy raises a powerful stew of emotions. Facilitated dialogue, an assortment of media, and a variety of exercises can help staff become more aware of the ways in which race, and the history of slavery, affect their own identities, and it can make them more aware of how to constructively approach their own emotions around slavery and race.

It is also essential that staff receive the training and expertise to navigate these conversations with the public, so that they are fully aware of the racial dynamics they are likely to encounter and be better equipped with a variety of techniques for helping visitors to manage their emotions and engage with the interpretation being offered. This means that staff must be familiar with basic concepts for understanding and discussing contemporary issues of race, such as those outlined in the first part of this chapter, and specific information about particular racial attitudes and dynamics that they are likely to encounter while interpreting slavery. Then staff can begin to learn how to work with these common attitudes and dynamics, through training in relevant interpretive techniques, such as open-ended questions—designed to help staff engage visitors based on their particular needs and interests—and facilitated dialogue, both of which may already have been introduced to staff in the first part of their training. Finally, practicing these techniques with one another, in a variety of interpretive scenarios, will not only deepen understanding and hone the skills that have been learned, but can provide interpreters with the experience necessary to allow them to be relaxed and confident in their encounters with the public.

In summary, when preparing front line staff to interpret slavery for the public:

1. Offer opportunities for staff to work through their own thoughts and feelings about race and racial identity before engaging with visitors.
2. Help staff to navigate the cognitive challenges, and the stew of emotions, raised by confronting historical narratives about slavery that may clash with those at the core of their own identities.
3. Offer staff training in understanding contemporary issues of race and about particular racial dynamics encountered when interpreting slavery.
4. Train staff in specific interpretive techniques, such as open-ended questions and facilitated dialogue, meant to engage visitors in exploring issues of slavery and race.
5. Provide staff with practice in using the skills they have learned in training with one another in order to strengthen interpretive skills and provide confidence and comfort.

Our website (www.tracingcenter.org) offers additional resources and suggestions for approaching this learning process, including books, articles, and films, and constructive ways to lead conversations about issues of race and the implications of the history of slavery for both staff and visitors.

Conclusion

If interpreters are not adequately prepared, they are likely to pass along many of their own feelings about slavery and race to their visitors. Without confronting their own biases in advance, interpreters also risk reproducing dominant historical narratives in which (1) the story of slavery is interpreted as the beginning and focus of black history; (2) white people are marginal to the story and black figures are largely passive actors; (3) slavery ultimately mattered little for the nation and its successes; (4) white people brought about emancipation, while black people were merely passive recipients of freedom.[17] Interpreting slavery without training in thinking through these issues can also lead to reinforcing our society's traditional divisions along racial lines, teaching black visitors that they are still seen as "the other." With historical context and a basic understanding of how racial dynamics have played out historically, interpreters can frame black enslavement as a painful yet inspirational story of human triumph and draw people closer to one another by exploring this shared history together.

Notes

1. This section draws on the work of Katrina Browne and James DeWolf Perry, of the Tracing Center on Histories and Legacies of Slavery in developing that organization's presentation of issues of race and racism.
2. Lincoln Quillian, "Does Unconscious Racism Exist?" *Social Psychology Quarterly* 71:1 (2008):6–11 (quotation at 11).

3. Cheryl Staats, "State of the Science: Implicit Bias Review 2013," with Charles Patton (Kirwan Institute, 2013), 27. Project Implicit runs an online version of the implicit association test at www.implicit.harvard.edu.
4. See Mark Peffley, Jon Hurwitz, and Paul Sniderman, "Racial Stereotypes and Whites' Political Views of Blacks in the Context of Welfare and Crime," *American Journal of Political Science* 41 (January 1997), 30–60.
5. Ira Katznelson, *When Affirmative Action Was White: An Untold History of Racial Inequality in Twentieth-Century America* (New York: W. W. Norton, 2005).
6. James Oliver Horton and Lois E. Horton, eds., *Slavery and Public History: The Tough Stuff of American Memory* (New York: New Press, 2006), 3.
7. *Traces of the Trade: A Story from the Deep North*, directed by Katrina Browne (Cambridge, MA: Ebb Pod Productions, 2008), DVD.
8. Katrina Browne, "The Psychological Consequences of Slavery for Beneficiaries of Slavery: Implications for Classroom Teaching," in *The Transatlantic Slave Trade and Slavery: New Directions in Teaching and Learning*, eds. Paul E. Lovejoy and Benjamin P. Bowser (Trenton, N.J.: Africa World Press, 2013), 219–44.
9. Diane J. Goodman, *Promoting Diversity and Social Justice: Educating People from Privileged Groups* (Thousand Oaks, Calif.: Sage, 2001), 70.
10. See, for instance, Tema Jon Okun, "The Emperor Has No Clothes: Teaching about Race and Racism to People Who Don't Want to Know" (Ph.D. dissertation, University of North Carolina at Greensboro, 2010), 103–5.
11. Browne, "Psychological Consequences of Slavery," 225–33.
12. Okun, "Emperor Has No Clothes," 105.
13. Browne, "Psychological Consequences of Slavery," 223.
14. Benjamin P. Bowser and Georges Goma-Gakissa, "Exploring Slavery's Influence on the Psychology of Slave Descendants in the United States," in Lovejoy and Bowser, *Transatlantic Slave Trade and Slavery*, 191, discussing the work of Ron Eyerman, especially Ron Eyerman, *Cultural Trauma: Slavery and the Formation of African American Identity* (New York: Cambridge University Press, 2001).
15. Alan J. Singer, *New York and Slavery: Time to Teach the Truth* (Albany: SUNY Press, 2008), 15.
16. Browne, "Psychological Consequences of Slavery," 234, 237.
17. Ibid., 236.

CHAPTER 3

"So Deeply Dyed in Our Fabric That It Cannot Be Washed Out"

Developing Institutional Support for the Interpretation of Slavery

LINNEA GRIM

SLAVERY AND its legacy are inextricably part of American history. And yet, for nearly a century, executive teams and boards of historic house museums curated tourist sites that memorialized prominent white men and erased all, or nearly all, vestiges of slavery.[1] Only within the past few decades have public history sites striven to find ways to evoke a holistic picture of the past. They are sponsoring scholarship, replacing passive language on signs with active, and creating public programs and events about slavery. These first steps have produced a directional change within the field. However, even these initial efforts, if carried out in isolation, may be superficial rather than transformative. Any long-term change from memorialization to inclusive history requires institutional support. When boards and executive teams foster this type of support for the interpretation of slavery, they make it central to planning, secure money and staffing for relevant initiatives, and create internal and external awareness. In this chapter, I will examine a variety of different sites interpreting slavery, focusing on the results of interviews with professionals—at Gunston Hall, Mount Vernon, and Monticello in Virginia, and at Philipsburg Manor in New York State—to illuminate ways in which historic site professionals are building institutional support for slavery interpretation.

My interviews with staff members at historic sites that have successfully navigated the process of making slavery an integral part of their interpretation show how staff and executive teams can take specific steps to initiate and sustain institutional support for this endeavor. In particular, historic sites and museums should consider doing the following: (1) acknowledge the difficulty and importance of the subject; (2) address its emotional impact; (3) find interpretation on both site-specific and contextual scholarship; (4) determine how interpreting slavery meets their missions; (5) craft thoughtful strategic and interpretive plans; (6) build networks of allies; (7) incorporate external advisory boards; and (8) use external publicity to their best long-term advantage.

Lessons for Institutional Support

1. Acknowledge the Difficulty and Importance of Interpreting Slavery

> This is tough stuff which ought not to be taken lightly. . . . The rest of social ills that derive from slavery and the depths of this problem in American culture today are not to be underestimated. And that's the vein you're tapping. . . . If you don't catch on to that and don't seek to channel your determination with grace and humanity, then I think you run the risk of just being controversial and flaming out.[2]

Effecting organizational change is always difficult.[3] It is even more challenging when tackling the interpretation of slavery, one of the most controversial and salient topics in our nation's history. Many visitors—and board and staff members—will have strong feelings about the significance and meaning of slavery. They won't all agree. Strong feelings mean that people find the topic important and relevant, whether they recognize this or not, and historic site and museum staff members need to be talking about it.

In a popular culture that often equates slavery with southern cotton plantations, one northern site has dedicated itself to providing a compelling story about slavery, Philipsburg Manor in Sleepy Hollow, New York (about 30 miles north of New York City).[4] Philipsburg Manor, administered by Historic Hudson Valley (HHV), is currently interpreted to 1750, the year that its absentee owner Adolph Philipse died. As Anglo-Dutch merchants, the Philipse family "rented land to tenant farmers of diverse European backgrounds and relied on a community of 23 enslaved Africans to operate the complex."[5] In the 1990s, staff members undertook a major reinterpretation project that focused the site's interpretation on slavery in the North. With grants from the National Endowment for the Humanities, the staff refocused the interpretation on the community of enslaved workers at the manor by incorporating reproduction artifacts and first-person programming that helped tell the community's story. Today, the staff remain committed to interpreting slavery: Waddell Stillman, president of HHV, says that interpreting slavery is now "so deeply dyed in our fabric that it cannot be washed out."[6]

Stillman credits the success of the reinterpretation of Philipsburg Manor to being cognizant of the significance of slavery interpretation. In 1994, the chair of the board at HHV pushed for a greater focus on slavery in the site's interpretation. Based on the reactions of other board members, Stillman learned about the hesitancies he and his staff would have

Figure 3.1. An interpreter at Philipsburg Manor in Sleepy Hollow, New York, leads visitors in a traditional dance at "Discover Pinkster!"—a cross-cultural festival.
Source: Bryan Haeffele.

to overcome to gain full board support. He said they learned they needed to "go slowly and develop the slavery story purposefully and carefully before reintroducing the topic to the public and to our own trustees.... We needed to do our homework."[7]

At George Washington's Mount Vernon, the interpretation and commemoration of the plantation's community has been a gradual process from the initial formal acknowledgment of the enslaved community in 1928, when the Mount Vernon Ladies' Association placed a memorial stone at the plantation's Slave Burial Ground, and the 1962 reconstruction of the Greenhouse Slave Quarters, to the active archaeology program and scholarly research. Some researchers have found that the inclusion of slavery interpretation has yet to comprehensively permeate the regular visitor experience. In her 2013 thesis on slavery interpretation at the homes of the first five US presidents, Amanda Seymour documented how staff members had marginalized slavery or portrayed it in benign ways at Mount Vernon. She found these issues in all aspects of the visitor experience from the introductory film to the house tour to interpretive signs to outdoor first-person interpretation.[8] Seymour concluded, "Generally changing the narrative from the happy or grateful slave/good master will require significant re-evaluation of the interpretive programming, but has the potential to considerably reshape understanding about American slavery, and by extension, the metanarrative of American history."[9] Some members of Mount Vernon's staff have begun thinking in a similar vein and are championing the significance of interpreting slavery at such an iconic American historical site.

When the curatorial staff recently decided to propose a special exhibit specifically focusing on the life of the enslaved on the estate, they were concerned how this would be received by the board. At a spring 2013 meeting of the board, the staff made their case, emphasizing why it is important to tell the story of the enslaved community now. According to Jessie MacLeod, assistant curator:

> First, the topic of slavery is of increasing interest to the American public as the nation grapples with the legacy of slavery and racial inequality. Second, Mount Vernon has access to unparalleled resources for telling the history of slavery in the Founding Era, including documents, objects, archaeological artifacts, architecture, and oral histories. Third, George Washington's estate is no longer in a leadership position among its peer institutions on the topic of slavery and risks falling behind if it does not adopt strategies to interpret slavery in innovative ways, following the example of Monticello, Montpelier, the Smithsonian, and other sites.[10]

When the staff demonstrated the relevancy of the exhibit, and an opportunity for the organization to demonstrate leadership in the field, the exhibition garnered board support and was approved.

Earlier chapters in this book have discussed the significance of the history of slavery in the United States and its resonance for modern visitors, including the reasons why this subject is today emotionally charged for, and even hotly disputed by visitors, staff, and board members alike. By explicitly addressing the reasons why the interpretation of slavery is vital for conveying the history of a site and the surrounding region, board and staff can gradually come to fully support a more robust interpretation of slavery. By taking the time to address the controversial issues at stake in interpreting slavery, meanwhile, your institution can avoid running into trouble as it proceeds to develop and implement new strategic plans. To navigate the subject of slavery with most board and staff will require taking the time to walk them through the emotional sensitivities involved in discussing slavery and race for themselves, for their colleagues, and for the site's visitors.

2. "The Fullness of Feeling": Address the Emotional Impact of Slavery on Staff and Visitors

Based on his experience at HHV, Stillman's paramount advice to staff members at other sites upon embarking on a program of slavery interpretation is this: "Channel determination into humanity and grace. [There's a] significant temptation to be provocative and to believe what you are doing is attention- and headline-grabbing. Sometimes we can be our own worst enemies with provocation.... Sometimes in that heat, the light is lost." He continues by saying that what he means by "humanity" in this context is "recognizing the fullness of feeling and the awkwardness and the shame and the pain to which [the history of slavery] points to in people's own lives and identity. To recognize that is to take enough time with it to respect the endeavor. [Interpreting slavery] is a human topic where people tap into depth of feeling and generations of guilt or shame. Those are big things to touch. You cannot touch those clumsily or without care."[11]

As Stillman identifies, talking about slavery comes with strong and varied emotional connections for people. Therefore, staff and board members who wish to maintain an ongoing, in-depth discussion about slavery with their audiences need first to address their own emotional connections to the topic and to open their minds to a vast array of multiple perspectives and reactions. Having staff and/or board members participate in a facilitated dialogue program about slavery and racial identity can be one effective way to accomplish this.

Perhaps no US historic site has more experience confronting the emotions raised by the topic of slavery than does Thomas Jefferson's Monticello.[12] Because of Jefferson's prominence in the founding of the United States and the extensive documentation of the Monticello plantation, scholars have examined slavery at Monticello for several decades. In-depth research on slavery at Monticello began through archaeological projects in the 1980s, which helped underpin some of the initiatives for recognizing the 250th anniversary in 1993 of Jefferson's birth.[13] At that time, an education task force identified interpreting slavery as a key opportunity. The Thomas Jefferson Foundation, which owns and operates Monticello, "could assume a position of leadership among historic sites in the interpretation of slave communities."[14] In the decades since, Monticello staff members have launched daily tours dedicated to slavery, special programs on the theme, a major traveling exhibition in partnership with the Smithsonian's National Museum of African American History and Culture—*Slavery at Jefferson's Monticello: Paradox of Liberty*—and are currently working on a restoration project along Mulberry Row, the center of industrial activity at the plantation, which will include the recreation of at least two slave sites.[15]

Prior to beginning their own facilitated dialogue program about slavery, a group of Monticello interpreters visited the Levine Museum of the New South to participate in a facilitated dialogue experience there. Monticello interpreters described later how important it was to their work to have participated in the facilitated dialogue experience. One stated that she realized "that slavery is not a shared experience for Americans, but a very individual one depending on individual frames of reference.... So when facilitating a conversation about slavery, or giving a tour, assumptions of [visitors'] knowledge or emotions cannot and should not be made."[16] Another interpreter explained that "our shared experience in Charlotte gave me much greater insight into how place and perspective informs the interpretive techniques of my colleagues.... I've learned to consider with every guest: 'where does this opinion come from,' but also to know that my assumptions are probably inaccurate. Whatever the issue, guests never fail to surprise me."[17] By beginning to examine their own connections to race and slavery through facilitated dialogue, the Monticello staff members were better prepared to offer ongoing programming about slavery from a position of comfort and confidence.

Another Monticello interpreter described the importance of using silence to create space for interpreters and visitors to process information.[18] A leading scholar on the interpretation of difficult history, Julia Rose, has offered advice along the same lines, marking the importance of finding the right space for having staff and board members wrestle with their own connections to slavery. She notes that staff members need to have both mental and physical space for this processing work. Specifically, she advises that the space be designed "for learning, safe from judgments yet supportive for constructive criticism.... An atmosphere of respect among museum workers and towards historical individuals is imperative."[19]

By having board and staff members wrestle with their own emotions surrounding slavery, they lay the groundwork for successful interpretation projects. Effective exhibitions and programs rest on knowing the needs and interests of intended audiences. Through reflecting on the emotional impact of slavery on themselves and others, staff members are better able to create nuanced messages and to meet people where they are. Furthermore, people sense when others are trying to hide their discomfort. In live interpretation, such situations can produce an escalation of emotion and a lack of feeling of safety. Through programs such as facilitated dialogues, staff and board members also learn to acknowledge explicitly the difficulty of this topic, thereby creating a more open learning environment for their guests. It is only through the investigation of one's own—and an acknowledgment of others'—connections to slavery and race in the United States that an interpreter can be ready to create an effective, ongoing conversation with visitors about the history and legacy of slavery.

3. Scholarship Is Key: Know the Context and the Specifics

Sustained institutional support rests upon scholarship that is both broad, providing the context for slavery in the United States, and specific to the history of a particular site. Scholarship not only continually feeds programming and exhibition topics, it also gives all staff members necessary information to feel confident in working with this difficult topic and to convey challenging material to visitors. Without knowing the historical context, it is harder for institutions and individual interpreters to answer visitors' overarching questions about slavery. Without the specifics related to the site, institutions can easily fall prey to generalizations that may not have been true for their sites, are devoid of the individual details and personal stories that visitors find compelling, and help portray to the public a monolithic, overly simplified picture of the history of slavery. Respondents in a Reach Advisor's study, "Connecticut Cultural Consumers," were almost unanimous in their feelings that "so long as the topic is mission appropriate, then history museums have almost a moral imperative to explore [difficult issues of the past]. And to not do so would undermine their trust in, and the authenticity of, that history museum."[20] In terms of institutional support, having a depth of scholarship can also help to assuage the doubts of staff and board members about embracing a sustained program on slavery. With the plethora of good literature on the history of slavery in the United States, it is relatively easy to create consistent training sessions for staff members that provide a contextual framework for the institution.

At Monticello, all new interpreters receive three hours of training focused solely on Monticello's enslaved community, with particular emphasis on incorporating slavery into the main house tour, weaving in the names and duties of those who worked in the house.

New interpreters also consider the historiography of slavery at Monticello and reflect on language choices, and on the variety of backgrounds and viewpoints of current visitors. In addition, those guides who choose to give "Slavery at Monticello" tours experience about sixteen hours of additional training, including a session, "Setting the Historical Context: How Does Slavery Come to the Piedmont," that provides a broad picture of the slave trade and its basis in the New World economy.

As at many sites, the evidence of slavery always existed at Philipsburg Manor, but it took several decades for the staff to take on the in-depth research that was needed. Adolph Philipse's probate inventory lists the names and some of the ages of twenty-three enslaved individuals, front and center, on the first page. Based on that document and the knowledge that Philipse spent the vast majority of his time in New York City, the staff began to research answers to questions such as "What was the work being done on Philipsburg? Who were these individuals? What skill level did they have to run a traditional plantation?"[21] The specifics and the context went hand in hand for the staff: "[Those questions] allowed us to explore the story of slavery in the Colonial North and the cultural and commercial development in New York ... and explain all the complicated issues that go around that."[22]

4. Hand in Glove: Determine How Interpreting Slavery Meets the Mission

In interviews with staff members for this chapter, no one remembered staff or board members explicitly arguing against interpreting slavery. Rather, the challenge was making the interpretation of slavery an institutional priority among all the other competing programs and initiatives. All sites should rely on their missions and visions to steer initiatives. Although statements do not necessarily need to explicitly mention slavery, they must recognize the importance of ideas and a holistic view of history rather than only supporting memorialization.

Gunston Hall, the home of statesman George Mason, is located in Mason Neck, Virginia, about 20 miles south of Washington, D.C. (figure 3.2)[23] Gunston Hall's history with the interpretation of slavery mirrors that of many other sites around the country. Over the years, they have made entrées into the topic—some first-person interpretation, a weekend dedicated to a black history theme, and some generic signs—but they have yet to create a sustained program to interpret slavery. Gunston Hall's executive director, Scott Stroh, said of most guests' current experience, "You're not given any opportunity to be aware of slave presence."[24] Through a recent strategic planning process, the staff and board are now ready to create sustained support for the interpretation of slavery at George Mason's estate.

Gunston Hall's revised mission statement thus provided the change in focus now helping the organization embrace a plan to tell the integrated history of Gunston Hall. The new mission statement language they crafted—"to stimulate continuing public exploration of democratic ideals as first presented by George Mason in the 1776 Virginia Declaration of Rights"—opens the door to subjects like slavery through the specific vehicle of Virginia's Declaration of Rights.[25] Stroh expounded, "Born out of that transition ... the Regents have fully embraced the issue of rights and then that has flowed into the issue of slavery."[26]

Monticello board and staff members similarly relied on changes in mission and vision statements to further their interpretation of slavery. Scholar Frank Cogliano described how

Figure 3.2. A docent takes high school students on a landscape tour through George Mason's garden at Gunston Hall.
Source: Frank N. Barker.

the Thomas Jefferson Foundation underwent a significant change in self-identity in the 1980s when the organization decided it was an academic institution, not merely a tourist attraction that memorialized Thomas Jefferson.[27] Dan Jordan, Monticello's new executive director at the time, came from an academic background and challenged the staff and board at Monticello to uphold the highest academic standards. Early in his tenure, the board adopted a new mission statement to reflect this commitment:

> Preservation: to conserve, protect, and maintain Monticello in a manner which leaves it enhanced and unimpaired for future generations and education: to interpret and present Thomas Jefferson to the widest possible audiences, including scholars and the general public.[28]

In 2009, the board of trustees adopted a vision statement to guide the foundation for the next several decades: "The Thomas Jefferson Foundation engages a global audience in a dialogue with Jefferson's ideas." In support of this vision, "The Foundation seeks to facilitate conversations and to use its extensive research and knowledge to stimulate interactions on a variety of topics that were of keen interest to Jefferson, the most powerful of which are liberty and self-government. Through virtual, off-site and on-site engagement, the Foundation seeks to excite the world about Jefferson's relevance today and ignite a passion for history."[29] Such statements directly influenced programming decisions, such as Monticello's first steps into a facilitated dialogue program, "Waiting on Liberty: Slavery at Jefferson's 'Great House,'" which debuted in 2012.

5. "More Ideas Than Resources": Craft Thoughtful Strategic and Interpretive Plans

Mission and vision statements set the stage for institutions to create strategic and interpretive plans. HHV has had its current mission statement since 1995: "The mission of Historic Hudson Valley is to celebrate the history, architecture, landscape, and material culture of the Hudson Valley, advancing its importance and thereby assuring its preservation."[30] Though broad, the mission shies away from big ideas. Within the framework of this mission, the staff members working on the Philipsburg Manor project felt they needed a stronger call to purpose. The staff and the African American Advisory Board (AAAB) set out two specific aspirational goals for the reinterpretation project through an interpretive plan:

1. Set the standard for interpreting enslavement in the northern colonies [and] enable visitors to better understand the varied individual relationships among slave, owner, and tenant, and the inseparable institutional relationships among enslavement, commerce, and culture.
2. Provide research materials necessary to academics, educators, and students of history for public discourse on the history and legacy of enslavement [and] spark interest in public history, provide an open environment for debate, and encourage new interpretive methods for presenting these and related issues to our visitors.[31]

These words did more than explain the goals of the reinterpretation process to those outside the institution. As Michael Lord, associate director of education at HHV, said, "We needed it to have these words for the staff to focus ourselves ... and to understand the direction we wished to go. This was very important as an internal document as much as it was to state our purpose."[32]

Gunston Hall is turning to strategic planning to ensure the importance of slavery interpretation as the site moves into the next several years. After revising the mission statement, the regents decided to wait to complete the strategic planning process until they had a new executive director in place. Once Scott Stroh had arrived, the staff, volunteers, a few state officials, and board members worked to finalize the new strategic plan. They wrestled with the best ways to meet their mission. Describing the lengthy process through which staff and board decided how to incorporate slavery into the strategic plan, Lacy Villiva, Gunston Hall's education manager, said they decided to make it clear in one of the plan's objectives: "Implement experiences interpreting slavery and the African American experience at Gunston Hall."[33]

Effective strategic and interpretive plans are important to securing institutional support for the interpretation of slavery because they create the road map and help determine the steps employees will take. Staying focused is particularly important when working with interpreting difficult knowledge. Because interpretating slavery is challenging to do well, staff members might be easily distracted by less daunting projects. Written plans help all staff stay focused on achieving their goals with minimal distractions and wrong turns. On a more concrete level, granting organizations and most individual donors need to see evidence that an organization knows where it is and where it is going, with written documentation of its priorities and ways to achieve them. As Lynda Jones, director of human resources at HHV, said, "We have far more ideas than resources. We have to wrestle ourselves down to focus on things that will get the biggest bang for the buck. There's never enough money."[34] Having and following thoughtful plans helps garner resources and then direct them as efficiently as possible.

6. "It's Who We Are": Build a Network of Staff and Board Allies to Create a Culture of Pride in Interpreting Slavery

The passion of a single staff or board member can launch an initiative, but sustained support will be imperiled if it rests on the shoulders of just one or two people. These sites demonstrate that having a network of board and staff allies is critical for building and maintaining successful programs. Having advocates ensures that efforts will not end when that particular enthusiastic staff or board member leaves.

At Mount Vernon, the staff of the archaeology, research, and preservation departments are closely aligned with the curatorial staff, creating a strong set of advocates for their exhibition about slavery on the estate. The majority of information about those enslaved by the Washingtons is revealed by the material culture from archaeological digs on the property and the close reading of letters, journals, newspapers, plantation records, and other primary sources, all of which the staff want to share with the public. The organization's development and marketing departments have also started working closely with the curatorial staff to raise money and awareness for the exhibit. One fundraising event, supported by a substantive donor group, yielded no negative feedback in relation to the exhibit but was also less successful in raising money than comparable events in previous years: "This disparity was likely due in part to the fact that the event supported research—a database of the enslaved community, archaeological excavations, and development of the slavery—rather than something more tangible like the conservation or acquisition of an object. It is also possible, however, that the topic of slavery did not find as receptive an audience among Mount Vernon's current pool of donors."[35]

Monticello's core group of staff members who implemented programs related to slavery at Monticello in the early 1990s included the foundation's president, Dan Jordan, and key senior staff members, including Lucia Stanton, Susan Stein, Dianne Swann-Wright, and Beth Taylor. Taylor, then director of interpretation, described the tremendous amount of passion they felt for interpreting the lives of the enslaved community at Monticello. She also noted her sense of pride in telling the histories of the enslaved community, especially through their efforts to recruit a more diverse workforce.[36] Stanton and Swann-Wright, two of the strongest staff advocates for research and dissemination of information related to slavery, labored for decades on researching the lives of the enslaved community at Monticello and their descendants through the "Getting Word" oral history project, and Stanton's published writings on slavery at Monticello, including the well-received books *Free Some Day* and *Those Who Labor for My Happiness*.[37]

Jordan, Stanton, Swann-Wright, and Taylor's departures in the past decade could have jeopardized the slavery interpretation program. However, the senior staff and board brought on new staff members who shared a passion for telling the histories of the enslaved community. Even though not all programs continued, fresh ones came to the fore. As new staff members joined the organization, including new president Leslie Greene Bowman, their passion and ideas helped Monticello pursue innovative opportunities. The major traveling exhibition *Slavery at Monticello: Paradox of Liberty* resulted from the friendship between Bowman and Lonnie Bunch, the director of the Smithsonian's National Museum of African American History and Culture. In the curatorial department, Susan Stein, Elizabeth Chew, Christa Dierksheide, Justin Sarafin, among others, led the way in communicating about Monticello's enslaved community through the traveling exhibition and new interpretive signs and exhibitions at Monticello.[38]

One way to foster a group of people dedicated to slavery interpretation is through the hiring process. During job interviews in the Education and Visitor Programs department, staff members at Monticello delve into the importance of interpreting slavery with candidates. As an example, all potential guides learn about the foundation's vision, namely, the intent to foster dialogue about Jefferson's ideas, along with specific topics, such as the relationship between Sally Hemings and Thomas Jefferson that produced six children, whom Jefferson enslaved. The interview panels take into account applicant responses to these questions determining whether candidates will be a good fit with Monticello's culture.

Gunston Hall is at a different stage in their development of a slavery interpretation program. Stroh described how a confluence of events helped ensure that slavery interpretation at Gunston Hall will continue to have broad support. During the strategic planning process, a work group was formed to look specifically at educational efforts and to decide what should be included in the plan. The work group consisted of staff, members of the community, including volunteer docents, and members of the board of regents. A core group consisting of two volunteers, one board member, and one community member championed slavery as a stand-alone part of the plan. In the past, several individuals had considered interpreting slavery important, but this small group was the first to champion it. Stroh believes that this small, organized group made it possible for others to join them and continue to spread enthusiasm for interpreting slavery.[39]

At HHV, Stillman recognized the importance of having many staff members dedicated to the reinterpretation project at Philipsburg Manor. They needed to feel that they were "participating in something bigger than ourselves." He noted that, though it is rewarding to have many of the same staff members who initially worked on the reinterpretation of Philipsburg still with the organization, he believes that they have created something that will outlast any one or two staff members. He explained, "For [slavery interpretation] to be part of our DNA, we need to have several strands of it," meaning several staff members committed to the same purpose.[40]

7. An Outside Lens: Rely on External Advisory Boards for Expertise and Accountability

An external advisory group can provide an alternate view of an organization's current efforts and a needed push when internal processes get bogged down. Staff members at HHV recognize the significance of their AAAB, which consulted on the reinterpretation of Philipsburg Manor and continues to work with them on current initiatives related to African American history.

The staff at HHV determined that they needed an advisory board when they considered the direction of their new interpretation. As Stillman said, "We were a white organization—with exception of the director of education [an African American woman] at the time—dealing with an African American story and we had no substantial African American voice."[41] The director of education, whose charge it was to integrate the story of slavery into HHV's education programs, was recruited by another institution soon after the school programs were implemented: "The school programs were our first programs to implement the new interpretation, as the students and their teachers were a very receptive audience, and we worked with adult learners in the general audience after we had our school programs implemented."[42] The staff recognized that they needed help from their local African American community to comprehensively tell the story of the enslaved workers. They called together a cross-section of African American community leaders to be a part of the AAAB.

Lynda Jones, now the director of human resources for HHV, first became associated with the organization through the AAAB. She described the excitement at the board's first meeting and her satisfaction to see that HHV was dedicated to getting the interpretation of slavery at Philipsburg Manor "right." She noted that the AAAB was active, meeting regularly as a large group and in smaller subcommittees, and taking part in staff training. Of their role, Jones said, "We advised on everything—how to present the information and what information was to be provided. We also debated whether the staff programming suggestions were a good way to deliver the message." The excitement felt on the first day continued throughout the process of reinterpretation and into the present. The AAAB still convenes to provide feedback on existing and upcoming programs.[43]

In terms of institutional support, Stillman said that the AAAB played a key role in fostering trustee and community buy-in. Because the staff and the AAAB built a strong relationship of trust, they were able to move through the process as a unit and rely on one another in communicating about the project. Jones and Lord say the trust resulted from constant communication and respect for the background and ideas that each staff and AAAB member brought to the meetings. Jones specifically mentions the importance of staff members incorporating their suggestions into program plans. Stillman said that the AAAB added substantially to the credibility of the efforts of the staff when presenting activities to the trustees.

Jones emphasized that the active involvement of Stillman, the president of the organization, with the AAAB was critical for providing institutional support for the reinterpretation project. She noted that he has never missed a meeting and has always been engaged fully in discussions. She said that the members of the AAAB have found his involvement energizing.[44]

For Mount Vernon's staff, their advisory panel, including historians, interpretive specialists, and descendants of the enslaved community, helped in two ways—general validation and specific cautionary advice: "First, the advisors confirmed that we *need* to do this exhibition now in order to do justice to the extraordinary resources available to us at Mount Vernon and to keep pace with the work of other institutions. Second, the advisors' comments reminded us of the myriad ways in which this subject matter is fraught and must be presented with care and sensitivity."[45] The ongoing relationship between the advisors and the staff is to continue throughout the exhibit development process, providing guidance, advice, and support for interpretation of Mount Vernon's enslaved community.

8. Media Spotlight: React to Publicity Purposefully; Harness It for Sustained Support

Governing boards and executive teams revel in good publicity and abhor the negative. Nevertheless, external publicity does make governing boards focus on the situation because they will pay attention when their site is in the spotlight of local or national media. Because of the gravity of the subject, and its emotional and often controversial nature, media reports often praise or excoriate historic sites for their attention and presentation of slavery.

Several staff members at these historic sites cautioned others to be wary of media reports that provoke boards and executive teams into making quick decisions that result in a superficial treatment of slavery. Negative newspaper publicity about Gunston Hall in 2000 sparked the board and staff to take quick action to post some signs related to George Mason's enslaved workforce. The staff now laments those signs because they were done in haste and reflect only a small amount of the history of slavery specific to Gunston Hall. They have carried this lesson forward to current planning. According to Stroh, some stakeholders, including a few individuals on the board, would like to see physical structures created quickly. He and the staff have learned from the past and have now dedicated resources to research, with an eye to reconstruction in the next few years rather than immediately.[46]

The significance of slavery and the potentially negative publicity its interpretation can bring causes hesitation among boards. Stillman explained that the controversy Colonial Williamsburg experienced in 1994, relating to its public program that reenacted a slave auction, had a cautionary effect on the board of trustees at HHV. He acknowledged that the board and staff of HHV were not seeking such headlines: "We had learned that we did not want to be in the paper as Colonial Williamsburg had been with its auction but we wanted to get to the same place."[47] In many ways, Stillman and the staff at HHV treated their reinterpretation program similarly to a capital campaign. They had a long, media-free quiet phase during which they did the necessary work to build the knowledge and support they needed. When they were ready, Stillman said that the board of trustees greeted the change with enthusiasm—and without fear of negative external publicity—because of the high level of scholarly support demonstrated through the NEH grants and community support shown by the advisory committee. Had there been any negative press, the board knew that there was a lot of careful and sustained planning that developed the reinterpretation.

On the positive side, media reports can help build popular awareness about what an institution has accomplished. Monticello staff members often face visitors who expect the site to glorify Jefferson and eschew slavery. Even though staff members have been proud of the work they have done related to slavery for the past two decades, conveying that to the public takes time. Monticello benefited from a number of national news stories related to the traveling exhibition *Slavery at Jefferson's Monticello: Paradox of Liberty*.[48] In the year following publicity related to the exhibition's opening at the Smithsonian, staff members heard on a regular basis that guests had come to Charlottesville to visit Monticello because of the exhibition. Additionally, the site has seen an increase in visitors attending its "Slavery at Monticello" tours.

Conclusion

Historic sites and museums find similar yet distinctive paths to securing institutional support for interpreting slavery. Staff members at Monticello began to build their program of interpreting slavery by linking in the organization's desire to be a scholarly institution. Philipsburg Manor, on the other hand, relied on the recognition they received from NEH grants and the collaborative work with their AAAB to construct the institutional support they needed for their reinterpretation project. Gunston Hall's staff and board have used the reshaping of the organization's mission to embrace the interpretation of slavery and allow them to finally tell the "whole story." Mount Vernon capitalized on their research and archaeological resources, and the institution's desire to be a leader in the field, to garner support for a special exhibit on the estate's enslaved community.

By following the steps that others have found successful—acknowledging the emotional impact, connecting slavery interpretation to mission, crafting thoughtful plans, depending on scholarship, building networks of allies, relying on advisory boards, and using publicity to our best advantage—we, as professionals, have the necessary building blocks to construct institutional support. This hard work is, in the end, well worth the investment of time and resources. The solid institutional foundation an organization develops ensures that its programs will endure.

Notes

1. Jennifer L. Eichstedt and Stephen Small, *Representations of Slavery: Race and Ideology in Southern Plantation Museums* (Washington, D.C.: Smithsonian Institution Press, 2002), 105–46.
2. Ibid.
3. Many authors have written on the challenges of change management. One of the best available resources is John P. Kotter, *Leading Change* (Boston: Harvard Business School Press, 1996).
4. Philipsburg Manor is administered by Historic Hudson Valley, a private, nonprofit entity governed by a board of trustees. The site receives about 55,000 visitors annually.
5. Historic Hudson Valley, "Philipsburg Manor." http://www.hudsonvalley.org/historic-sites/philipsburg-manor (accessed January 26, 2014).

6. Waddell Stillman, (president, Historic Hudson Valley), interview by the author, December 18, 2013.
7. Ibid.
8. Amanda G. Seymour, "Pride and Prejudice: The Historic Interpretation of Slavery at the Homes of Five Founding Fathers" (M.A. thesis, George Washington University, 2013), 23–34.
9. Ibid., 78.
10. Jessie MacLeod (assistant curator, George Washington's Mount Vernon), e-mail to the editor, May 31, 2014.
11. Ibid.
12. Monticello is owned and operated by the Thomas Jefferson Foundation, a private, nonprofit entity governed by a board of trustees. The site welcomes approximately 440,000 visitors each year.
13. Elizabeth V. Chew, "Institutional Evolution," *Museum* (September-October 2013). https://onlinedigeditions.com/article/Institution+Evolution/1481141/0/article.html (accessed January 26, 2014).
14. Thomas Jefferson Memorial Foundation, Master Plan 1988–1993, April 1988, 207.
15. "Monticello to Receive $10 Million Gift for Restoration Efforts." Thomas Jefferson Foundation press release, April 20, 2013, on the Monticello website. http://www.monticello.org/site/press/monticello-to-receive-10-million-gift-restoration-efforts (accessed January 26, 2014).
16. Harriet Resio (historic interpreter, Thomas Jefferson Foundation), e-mail to the author, March 3, 2014.
17. Brandon Dillard (historic interpreter, Thomas Jefferson Foundation), e-mail to the author, March 2, 2014.
18. David Ronka (manager of special programs, Thomas Jefferson Foundation), e-mail to the author, March 2, 2014.
19. Julia Rose, "What We Mean by 'Institutional Support.'" Presentation as part of the workshop "Giving Voice to the Long-Silenced Millions: Best Practices for Interpreting Slavery at Historic Sites and Museums" at the annual meeting of the American Association of State and Local History, Birmingham, Alabama, September 18–21, 2013.
20. Susie Wilkening, "Difficult Issues in History Museums," *Finding Community* (blog), December 9, 2013. http://findingcommunityengagingaudiences.blogspot.com/.
21. Michael Lord (associate director of education, Historic Hudson Valley), interview by the author, December 18, 2013.
22. Ibid.
23. Gunston Hall is owned by the Commonwealth of Virginia, is administered by the National Society of the Colonial Dames of America, and has an annual visitation of approximately 25,000 people.
24. Scott Stroh (executive director, Gunston Hall), interview by the author, September 6, 2013.
25. Ibid.
26. Ibid.
27. Francis D. Cogliano, "Preservation and Education: Monticello and the Thomas Jefferson Foundation," in *A Companion to Thomas Jefferson*, ed. Francis D. Cogliano (Malden, Mass.: Wiley-Blackwell, 2012), 515–18.
28. Ibid., 516.
29. Thomas Jefferson Foundation, "Mission Statement," Monticello website. http://www.monticello.org/site/about/mission-statement (accessed January 26, 2014).

30. Historic Hudson Valley, "Our Mission," HHV website. http://www.hudsonvalley.org/about, (accessed May 25, 2014).
31. Historic Hudson Valley, "Interpretive Plan for Philipsburg Manor, Upper Mills, Sleepy Hollow, New York," November 2003, 8.
32. Lord, interview.
33. "Gunston Hall Strategic Plan 2014–2018: Executive Summary," October 4, 2013, 5.
34. Lynda Jones (director of human resources, Historic Hudson Valley), interview by the author, December 18, 2013.
35. Jessie MacLeod (assistant curator, George Washington's Mount Vernon), e-mail to the editor, May 31, 2014.
36. Elizabeth D. Taylor, (former director of interpretation, Thomas Jefferson Foundation), interview by the author, 25 October 2013.
37. Lucia C. Stanton, *Free Some Day: The African-American Families of Monticello* (Thomas Jefferson Foundation, 2000); Lucia C. Stanton, *"Those Who Labor for My Happiness": Slavery at Thomas Jefferson's Monticello* (Charlottesville: University of Virginia Press, 2012).
38. Chew, "Institutional Evolution."
39. Stroh, in discussion with the author, March 3, 2014.
40. Stillman, interview.
41. Ibid.
42. Waddell Stillman, (president, Historic Hudson Valley), e-mail to the author, May 27, 2014.
43. Jones, interview.
44. Ibid.
45. Jessie MacLeod (assistant curator, George Washington's Mount Vernon), e-mail to the editor, May 31, 2014.
46. Stroh, interview.
47. Stillman, interview.
48. For example, Edward Rothstein, "Life, Liberty and the Fact of Slavery," *New York Times*, January 26, 2012. http://www.nytimes.com/2012/01/27/arts/design/smithsonian-and-monticello-exhibitions-on-jefferson-slaves.html (accessed on January 26, 2014); Jacqueline Trescott, "Closer Look at Jefferson's Slaves," *Washington Post*, January 27, 2012. http://www.washingtonpost.com/gog/exhibits/slavery-at-jeffersons-monticello-paradox-of-liberty,122311.html (accessed on January 26, 2014).

CHAPTER 4

Institutional Change at Northern Historic Sites

Telling Slavery's Story in the Land of Abolition

KATHERINE D. KANE

> The past is with us always, but we need to live with it, open our eyes and poke around in it, take it all in: the good, the bad and the mythic, if we want to stay connected to the ever-changing present.
>
> —*Peter Birkenhead*[1]

POKING AROUND in the past stirs things up. Telling slavery's history is important in the whole United States, and particularly important in the Northeast, which is proud of its abolitionist roots. Some in the North feel morally superior, gathering apocryphal Underground Railroad stories, expressing pride in abolitionist ancestors, and ignoring slavery's impact around them. But the northeastern United States wasn't just complicit in slavery: this part of the country played a leading role in the economic system based on slavery. As responsible history organizations, our job is to present comprehensive history. In the Northeast, that includes the facts and legacy of slavery. Professional ethical standards and the public trust within which we work demand nothing less.[2]

Bringing new and challenging content, such as slavery and its history, into an organization's interpretation means more than just reinterpretation, it means organizational change. Therefore, I posed the following questions in my case studies: How do we transform ourselves and our organizations to incorporate these stories into our narratives? How do we accomplish a shared institutional commitment to an interpretation contrary to what board and staff members may believe about their site? Awareness of the effort it takes to transform makes the reinterpretation more successful and more likely to stick. Sites with a history of slavery, including northern sites, can struggle with incorporating slavery's history into their narrative, and sites that have tackled this transformation have valuable lessons to share.

Organizational change is complex and difficult, requiring reflection, interaction, and committed leadership. Change agents—those individuals (internal and external) who champion and guide change—and stakeholder involvement (or lack of it) can make or break the transformation. Persistence, patience, and perseverance help. Fear of change builds resistance and reduces success. Change can be chaotic, painful, or unsuccessful; it disrupts relationships and power structures. There are practices that can assist with successful organizational transformation, including crafting a compelling vision and strategy, generating a shared commitment and sense of urgency, building a team dedicated to change, and institutionalizing the change.[3] Multiple perspectives and various points of view broaden impact of the transformation (see chapter 3, "'So Deeply Dyed in Our Fabric That It Cannot Be Washed Out': Developing Institutional Support for the Interpretation of Slavery").

Transforming interpretation to include slavery, at a historic site in the North or elsewhere, involves changing the institution's *culture* and reshaping the organization's values and mission to align with the historic content. "Culture" refers to the organization's shared understandings and practices. Key constituencies, including board, staff, donors, and other key players, have shared understandings about the history the site interprets (and does not interpret), the values the site represents, and the interpretive goals. All of these understandings may be threatened by including the history of slavery at a site where it has been absent or underrepresented. Institutional transformation must include educating all constituencies about the history of slavery in the North at the site and using facilitated dialogue and other techniques to help participants internalize what can be new information challenging their existing beliefs.

From Myth to Truth

The history of slavery in the North is hidden right in front of us. Slave economy prosperity can be seen in lovely homes around New England town greens, in substantial public buildings, and at prestigious institutions.[4] Even without direct ownership of human property, entire communities were complicit in the slave economy.[5] In Bristol, Rhode Island, white individuals of all classes bought shares in slave-trading voyages, financially benefiting from the ventures. The myth that the North was the land of freedom and the South the home of slavery ignores the facts, promotes misperceptions and stereotypes, and fosters subtle racism and amnesia regarding the region's history of slavery.[6] In eighteenth-century New England, large populations of enslaved people lived in port cities and were scattered throughout inland agricultural communities. These enslaved men and women were skilled tradespeople, domestic servants, and laborers, participants in the global maritime and commercial trades of the northern colonies. Many Americans today are unfamiliar with northern slavery. If they are aware of it at all, they have likely accepted the corollary myths that northern slavery was more limited in scope and somehow milder and kinder than the southern variety, perpetuating a double standard.

Nonprofit history organizations are responsible to their publics. Trusted when public distrust of other institutions is high, museums must live up to that assurance. Sharing the entire story is an ethical responsibility. Discomfort, fear, resistance, and anger may arise, but they can be faced with patience, open-mindedness, and courage. The work of telling slavery's story is difficult and uncomfortable, so we must encourage one another. And our audiences have changed: no longer expecting passive lectures or simplistic information, they are interested in complex history with challenging implications and are looking for opportunities to learn and to reflect.[7]

Many northern museums are influencing one another, such as the New-York Historical Society, Philipsburg Manor, and the Weeksville Heritage Society, to name just a few, with their interpretations of enslavement and freedom. Using five organizations as examples, I'll examine their change processes, what drove those processes, who was involved, their impact and barriers encountered, whether changes have "stuck," and I'll offer what I hope are some useful conclusions.

Case Studies

Mattatuck Museum: Restoring Personhood to a Long-Forgotten Man

Founded in 1877, the Mattatuck Museum in Waterbury, Connecticut, "is a center of art and history, a gathering place that nurtures creativity and learning through transformative experiences to encourage a deeper understanding of ourselves and our heritage."[8]

The impetus for the Mattatuck Museum to interpret slavery was an articulated skeleton exhibited at the museum for many years known as "Larry" (a name branded in ink across his forehead).[9] In reality, this was the eighteenth-century skeleton of a man known as "Fortune," who was enslaved in Waterbury, along with his family, by Dr. Preserved Porter. Fortune and his wife, Dinah, registered their children's births under Connecticut's 1784 gradual emancipation law, but in reality, their children were likely sold after Fortune's death. Porter bequeathed Dinah to his widow, who then sold her. Whether by their own actions or the vicissitudes of slavery, Fortune's wife and children disappeared from the historical record, their descendants unknown.

Fortune died in 1798 at about sixty, old for his time, but, judging by his remains, still strong. Porter, an orthopedist, processed Fortune's body, preserving his bones and marking them for identification and anatomical study. The Porters, many of them physicians, possessed Fortune's bones for four more generations. After receiving Fortune's remains as a donation in 1933, the museum assembled the bones into an articulated skeleton for display.

Prompted by community demands, Fortune's remains were removed from exhibit in 1970. The museum embarked on a twenty-five-year collaborative journey when the museum's partner, the African American History Project Committee, chaired by Maxine Watts, proposed learning about the remains. The committee and museum conducted extensive research, recruited historians and physical anthropologists, built an exhibit (on-site and online), and presented papers, programs, and teacher institutes. Fortune's bones were comprehensively examined, and the results indicate that he was strong, conducted hard work, and suffered injuries. A forensic artist illustrated what Fortune may have looked like. Marilyn Nelson, Connecticut's poet laureate, was commissioned to write a poem, "Fortune's Bones: The Manumission Requiem."[10]

Ultimately, the committee and museum decided that Fortune should be properly buried. In the fall of 2013, he was interred after lying in state in the rotunda of the Connecticut State Capitol and being eulogized at a service at St. John's Episcopal Church, where he was baptized the year before he died. "The museum did not do any research on who he really was, how he died, what he did. He was just there as an attraction," said Marie Galbraith, director of the Mattatuck from 2001 to 2012. "Now the research has been done. We did as much as we can. We want to give Fortune his personhood."[11] "Fortune was in storage for 30 years," Maxine Watts said. "We brought him up, resurrected him. We were responsible for him. This slave proved after 200 years, we're all the same under our skin."

Analysis

The African American History Project Committee was the driving coalition and the change agent behind this project at the Mattatuck Museum. The museum had to adapt to uncomfortable information and to recognize its own complicity. The two groups already had a partnership and working relationship to build upon. Institutional change was gradual. They built relationships with scholars, shared the research with the community, and listened to the reactions. This research shaped their actions. Shocked to learn the details, many individuals worked to bring Fortune's story forward. Fortune's life and suffering were present in his bones. He was one person representing all the enslaved people of eighteenth-century Waterbury, but his tangible remains were there in front of them, so the research went beyond words on brittle old paper.

The museum maintains a permanent installation and an extensive companion website to tell Fortune's story and the history of slavery in the community. The museum's strategic plan lists "fostering strong relationships with our community" as a core value, and the museum continues to welcome members of the community to participate in their African American History Project Committee, which advises the museum on interpretation and community-based exhibits.[12] Their *Coming Home* exhibit about Waterbury's history includes stories about the city's African American and Jewish communities.[13]

Linden Place: The Legacy of Slave Traders

Linden Place is a historic mansion in Bristol, Rhode Island, "built in 1810 by the seafaring General George DeWolf"; thus does the Linden Place website introduce the site's history.[14] In fact, George DeWolf's business was the slave trade, and he is said to have built the mansion with the profits from a single year of his illegal slave-trading. George was the nephew of US Senator James DeWolf, who is regarded as the most prolific slave trader in the history of the United States. Collectively, James, George, and the extended DeWolf family brought more than 12,000 Africans across the Middle Passage to enslavement in the United States and the Caribbean, and the true number, including unrecorded illegal

Figure 4.1. Filmmaker and DeWolf descendant Katrina Browne in front of Linden Place, the historic home of George DeWolf, a member of the nation's leading slave-trading family in the early nineteenth century.
Source: Alla Kovgan.

voyages, is probably far higher: "Over fifty years and three generations, from 1769 to 1820, the DeWolfs were the nation's leading slave traders."[15]

Out of tiny Bristol, Rhode Island, the DeWolf family built their vast wealth with rum, textiles, sugar, and slaves. This family enterprise, however, is merely the most prominent example of New England's deep involvement in the transatlantic slave trade. Linden Place represents the trade, how it permeated life in Rhode Island and throughout New England, and the widespread resistance to remembering that history. Occupied by eight generations, then purchased with state help by the nonprofit Friends of Linden Place, it opened as a museum in 1990. The museum supports five buildings and 2 acres with house tours, children's programs and lectures, and a lively wedding business: "It is the mission of the Friends of Linden Place to restore and preserve its treasured historic property and to insure its public accessibility by developing a program of uses that will enhance the artistic, cultural and educational life of the community."[16] Interpretation focuses on the celebrity, drama, and glamour of the many generations of the DeWolf family. Staff and board have been reluctant to interpret slavery and have expressed the concern that public response could physically damage the house. But in recent years, external factors, including Brown University's report, "Slavery and Justice," on that university's historical connections with slavery and the slave trade, have offered examples of change the museum could use to support its own work.

In 2001, DeWolf family members, organized by descendant Katrina Browne, began exploring their family's slave-trading history. Ten DeWolf descendants retraced their family's slaving voyages from Linden Place to the coast of Ghana to the ruins of a DeWolf slave plantation in Cuba. The resulting 2008 PBS documentary, *Traces of the Trade: A Story from the Deep North*, pushes beyond the family's story to explore the legacy of slavery in the North and issues of white privilege. The film won several awards and an Emmy Award nomination for original research.[17] Since being broadcast on national television, the film has spawned a nonprofit, the Tracing Center on Histories and Legacies of Slavery, offering programs on this history, its implications for racial privilege and equity, and several books.[18]

As described in the film, the board of Linden Place declined to work with the filmmakers. The museum had no filming policies, and at a site where people are proud of the architecture and the prominent DeWolf family, there were worries that the documentary would be polemical. When released, however, the film broke barriers and got people talking. Slavery was "in the open. That made it easier," said Jim Connell, executive director of Linden Place.

In response to these changes, in 2012 Linden Place began offering a walking tour of Bristol and its connections to the slave trade, beginning at the mansion and concluding with a rum drink at the DeWolf Tavern, formerly a wharf warehouse owned by James DeWolf. The tour offers a good deal of information about the town's complicity, but it does not include opportunities for discussion or reflection.

This walking tour is presented six to eight times a year, and its capacity for twenty-five guests always sell out. The participants are mostly white, and there has been no evaluation process to learn why they sign up for the tour, or what they think of it afterward. Robin Tremblay, Linden Place's office manager, prepared the tour, funded by the Rhode Island Council for the Humanities. Currently the sole presenter, Tremblay expects to train volunteer docents soon. Linden Place is trying to recruit an African American guide, hoping that this will increase community engagement and attract more African American visitors. Recruitment efforts have, however, been unsuccessful.

Linden Place has added to its repertoire material interpreting slavery; however, the walking tour experience interprets slavery separately from the rest of the mansion's story, and any connection of the mansion or the DeWolf family to slavery is scarcely visible to the average visitor. Connell is proud of Linden Place's "Africana" programs: the walking tour and periodic lectures. Though lack of time and money affects implementation, they plan to exhibit James DeWolf's 1821 coach, "one of the rarest, and nicest, historic coaches,"[19] with information on the triangle trade, content not dependent on interpreters.

Analysis

Linden Place has approached interpreting slavery incrementally and carefully. They have responded to the growing public conversation about slavery but have not integrated their resulting research into the overall site interpretation. The walking tour, the focus of these efforts, consistently sells out, but it is offered infrequently and remains dependent upon a single tour guide. What else might Linden Place do, subject to time and resource constraints, to improve its interpretation of slavery? The walking tour could spend more time in the mansion, connecting its occupants to slavery and the slave trade in Bristol. They could survey tour participants, evaluating the tour's effectiveness and assessing what visitors would like to learn and how they would like to learn it. They could incorporate information on slavery into regular house tours, presenting more stories about the original inhabitants of the mansion, their slaving voyages, and the broader context of the world these individuals occupied.

Linden Place would like to attract more African American visitors and views the slavery walking tour as a means to do so. Though an African American tour guide might help with this goal (and could also be a valuable part of a team dedicated to change), white staff or volunteers interpreting slavery are hardly unusual or inadequate. To build community involvement and attract African American visitors, Linden Place could seek community input and involvement, add African American members to the board and staff, and recruit community advisors whose suggestions are accorded respect.

Linden Place is a prime example of a northern historic site where the interpretation of slavery in connection with the site and the surrounding community has been a sensitive topic among stakeholders. Institutions in this situation must proceed carefully and deliberately and lay the groundwork for changes in interpretation. For change, there must be interest. For staff, board, or community members familiar with a site where they believe the comprehensive history is ignored, they must act strategically and sometimes subversively by publicly asking questions regarding content, audience, and funding; by presenting public (or board) programs using varied historic content and voices, and by engaging the community in a collaborative learning process; by developing community advisory groups; and by using strategic planning to drive change for a deliberative internal process. Appropriate steps can include training board, staff, and volunteers with historical information while implementing specialized training and facilitated dialogue on how to discuss this information sensitively. This process could help develop community support for interpreting slavery, integrating community voices into planning and implementation, building trust and accountability for the site's interpretation, and enhancing staff confidence in offering this history to visitors. Through relationships with scholars and experts on race, and with the larger community, gathering audience input on current programs and bringing varied points of view to the table, interpretive content at a site like Linden Place can be enlivened, expanded, and made more relevant, accompanied by increased visibility and revenue growth.

Royall House and Slave Quarters: Reimagining an Institution

A 1750 visitor to Royall House, among formal gardens and 500 agricultural acres in Medford, Massachusetts, called it "one of the grandest houses in North America."[20] The Royall family were immensely wealthy thanks to the slave trade and Caribbean sugar grown and processed by people they enslaved. The property had been acquired in 1732 by merchant Isaac Royall, who brought with him his family and twenty-seven enslaved people from Antigua. In his 1781 will, Royall's son, Isaac Jr., used his family's wealth to endow chairs in law and medicine at Harvard, which resulted in the establishment of both Harvard Medical School and Harvard Law School.[21]

At the dawn of the American Revolution, the loyalist Royalls left the colonies, and the house headquartered colonial generals Lee, Stark, and Sullivan. Because of these Revolutionary War associations, the Friends of the Royall House was founded and the house restored by

Figure 4.2. A study in contrasts—the front and back stairs of Royall House.
Source: Katherine D. Kane.

members of the Daughters of the American Revolution in the early twentieth century, operating as a classic house museum with the genteel story of the Royall's home and American independence. Yet all this time, there was another building only 35 feet from the main house, which is likely the only surviving slave quarters in the northeastern United States.

In the late twentieth century, Royall House transformed from polite Colonial Revival interpretation to a more robust story—the grand eighteenth-century home of the largest slaveholders in Massachusetts. Along with this change in interpretation, the site altered its name to Royall House and Slave Quarters (RHSQ). Board member Gracelaw Simmons says, "The story was always there, hiding in plain sight." Tom Lincoln, executive director of RHSQ, observes that if they weren't interpreting slavery, they'd be remiss.

This change began in the 1990s as research about the site and people associated with it accumulated. Royall House built relationships with local universities and appointed an academic council of prominent scholars and museum specialists. Boston University archaeological excavations recovered 5,000 pre-Revolutionary artifacts and fragments, many of them tangible evidence of enslaved people.

Research revealed details about individuals enslaved by the Royalls. Belinda was captured as a girl and enslaved for fifty years. When freed upon Isaac Royall Jr.'s death, she was elderly and responsible for an infirm daughter. Petitioning the Massachusetts General Court for a pension from the Royall's estate, whose wealth was "accumulated by her own industry" and "augmented by her servitude," she was awarded 15 pounds 5 shillings annually, but she had to return to court because it was only paid once.[22] Belinda's fight gives her identity and agency when enslaved people are often portrayed as a nameless, faceless group. Her story provides richness and depth to the RHSQ site and narrative, and it presents an interesting counterpoint to the comfortable lives of the Royalls.

Change continued at Royall House in the 2000s as older donors passed away, new board members were recruited, and support in the community broadened. Newcomers weren't invested in the old decorative arts stories, or in Yankee and Colonial Revival myths. A Royall family descendant joined the board, willing to acknowledge the family story. The board realized that eighteenth-century houses are not rare in Massachusetts, that they needed to find their niche, that public interests had changed—and they understood they were responsible for telling the whole story of the site under their care,

The museum has an annual budget of about $50,000 and one part-time employee, so strategic planning was critical for transformation. The site reframed its mission to be more inclusive: the museum "explores the meanings of freedom and independence before, during and since the American Revolution, in the context of a household of wealthy Loyalists and enslaved Africans."[23]

Extraneous artifacts were removed from the house and spaces reinstalled so that visitors can see evidence of the presence of enslaved people, such as the back stairway they used (figure 4.2) and the rooms it connects, along with a second-floor kitchen chamber across from the master chamber, reinterpreted from a description in Isaac Royall's estate inventory. "We call it bounty and bondage," says Simmons. "You see most dramatically how closely the two resident populations lived with each other. An elegant bedroom for the Royalls was across the hall from a storage room that enslaved people slept in."

The interpretation of the slave quarters now includes exhibits describing the historic landscape and archaeological excavations, illustrating where enslaved people worked. RHSQ changed tour and volunteer guide training, conducted an NEH teacher institute, and is developing new school curricula. Programs are more focused and compelling, less "English Country Houses in America" and more "Slavery and the Politics of Memory in Massachusetts."

Rightly proud of their accomplishments, the institution believes that each step has raised its credibility. They have formed relationships with other sites interpreting slavery, used research, generational change, academic relationships, and reflection to transform their organization, and have employed a strategic plan to focus the organization. Where most members were once from a single ZIP code, now the site's reach extends well beyond the local community. There are more African American visitors. An expanded website draws visitors, group tours are up, and the institution has garnered additional foundation support.

The transformation of RHSQ continues. Even with reinstalled spaces, the house tour itself remains primarily focused on the elite family and their home and possessions. With one exception, enslaved individuals are not present, but several Royall family members are discussed. The slave quarters have become a multi-use space for programs, ticket sales, and a museum store, so that the space where enslaved people lived and worked is treated very differently than the mansion, still graciously presented as a lovely home, a museum. The surrounding landscape is twentieth-century-style lawn without wear. The slave quarters building is a substantial and well-preserved two stories; as a result, visitors may conclude that conditions for enslaved people were good. Pragmatic decisions of a small museum, these choices make it difficult for visitors to imagine the people who lived here and risk confusing the museum's messages.

The organizational shift has also changed those associated with Royall House. Board member Gracelaw Simmons says she now sees slavery's impact everywhere, "but people want to ignore it; the work of the Royall House is to open people's eyes."

Analysis

Despite being a small organization, RHSQ has become a leader in the interpretation of northern slavery. Their process began with the commitment and vision of a handful of individuals, but all constituencies were educated, involved, and brought on board with a shared vision for institutional transformation. Comprehensive historical research was conducted early in the process to lay a solid foundation for interpretation and for transforming institutional culture so the new historical interpretation aligns with a new set of institutional goals and values. A wide variety of community partners participated in the transformation and supported it. Fundraising provided critical resources for the new vision and institutional goals. Strategic planning has continued, and RHSQ has become a prominent destination for scholars, activists, and others interested in the history of slavery and race in New England and the implications of this history for contemporary life.

The Harriet Beecher Stowe Center and Cliveden: Different Histories, Parallel Changes

Harriet Beecher Stowe's *Uncle Tom's Cabin* (1852) was an unexpected international best seller and changed American attitudes about slavery but, transplanted onto the stage and stripped of the book's antislavery and feminist content, the title character was transformed into a stereotyped racial slur. Today, *Uncle Tom's Cabin* is read around the world. The programs of the Harriet Beecher Stowe Center, the historic house museum in Hartford, Connecticut, where Stowe lived for twenty-five years, recognize that discussing Stowe and her best-known book inevitably means discussing difficult issues of slavery and race. This challenge also represents an opportunity to connect historic programs and contemporary issues: What can we do today about racism? Bullying? Inequity?

This wasn't always the case at the Stowe Center. Opened in 1968, the museum was declining by the late 1990s. Today, the center is financially stable, with an internationally recognized story and a diverse board of trustees, and it has found a niche in the crowded New England museum market. This transformation was guided by strategic planning, and revisions in interpretive content were led by a restated mission: The Stowe Center "preserves and interprets Stowe's Hartford home and the Center's historic collections, promotes vibrant discussion of her life and work, and inspires commitment to social justice and positive change."[24]

In 2008, the center initiated an award-winning series of dialogue-based "parlor conversations," called "Salons at Stowe," to bring people together to discuss contemporary issues, such as human trafficking, stereotyping, and issues of race and gender. Program themes have leveraged historic anniversaries related to slavery and emancipation. The center bestows the Stowe Prize for Writing to Advance Social Justice, a biannual award recognizing a writer whose publications align with the museum's mission. Staff recruitment and training now include discussing challenging content, mentoring feedback, storytelling techniques, and field trips to other places presenting challenging content.

Cliveden, a 1767 colonial home in Philadelphia, "has long had an air of mystery ... its history related to slavery and domestic servitude was known but remained hidden."[25] Cliveden recently conducted a strategic reinterpretation, changing its focus from revolutionary era history, architecture, and decorative arts to a community-developed narrative focused on slavery and its impact on all Americans.[26]

In the 1990s, when the Historical Society of Pennsylvania processed the papers of the Chew family, Cliveden's owners for seven generations, they were finally recognized as among the largest slave-owning families in the Philadelphia region. In 2010, Cliveden began "to emancipate the stories long hidden in the archives [and] transform the institution."[27] Cliveden began an innovative program, turning into a place where community members discuss uncomfortable questions about race, class, and power: "Cliveden's mission is to help people understand our shared history and motivate them to preserve it by providing access to the rich continuity of history and preservation in one community and family over time, and by offering direction and knowledge about preserving our built heritage and its value."[28]

Cliveden organized board retreats, charrettes, panels, and community conversations to discuss issues and establish goals and measures. The site's interpretation now explains how slavery worked, outlines its legacies of wealth, racism, and historical amnesia, and illustrates resistance to slavery. Leadership from the board, staff, and community was critical to reaching this point. Author Edward W. Robinson "helped teach Cliveden's staff ways to avoid 'shame and blame' so that the stories of individuals would showcase empowerment and active agency."[29]

Cliveden rolled out its new interpretation in 2012 with an exhibit, a website, and programs "telling the whole story in ways that allow visitors to question their assumptions about American history by examining its many contradictions."[30] "Cliveden Conversations," like "Salons at Stowe," is a series of conversations on race, history, and memory. Philadelphia Young Playwrights developed *Liberty to Go to See*, interactive performances with the Chews and their enslaved, indentured, and free servants.[31] A film, *Emancipating Cliveden*, introduces visitors to the process of recovering and reinterpreting the site's history.

Analysis

At both the Stowe Center and Cliveden, board and staff members developed a compelling vision and forged a guiding coalition. They were thoughtful and reflective. Most importantly, they integrated multiple perspectives and various points of view, broadening their impact.

At both sites, recognition, attendance, and revenue are up, audiences are more diverse, and the community is deeply involved. Cliveden was featured in the American Historical Association's *Perspectives on History*,[32] and Stowe staff have been invited to discuss its programs at national and international meetings. "Salons at Stowe" has won awards and international attention.

These changes have not been easy. Grappling with challenging content initially meant staff and board turnover at Stowe, because only some individuals decided to align with the new mission and content, some thought it a mistake to discuss contemporary issues, and others thought that the center wasn't going far enough. At Cliveden, some community members pushed back, charging racism or arguing that white-founded Cliveden was taking over African American history. These effects of change remind us it's important to connect with a wide range of community members early in the process, because those in the community who push back have valid perspectives, and community involvement builds trust, authenticity, legitimacy, and accountability.

At the Stowe Center, the process of institutionalization is not complete. For instance, the interpretive philosophy is not yet well reflected in Stowe House tours. Cliveden's process has been more compressed, and institutionalization is still under way.

Concluding Thoughts

Each of these museums has worked within their circumstances—geography, history, and institutional culture—to make change. Yet circumstances can be both liberating and limiting. Since change can make us uncomfortable, disrupting relationships and power structures, the process often provokes resistance and fear. These case studies show how easy it can be to underestimate the effort involved in seeking transformational change and how an insufficiently articulated vision or internal cultural shift can result in a less than satisfactory outcome. Yet there are reasons for us to be optimistic in looking at the stories of these northern sites. For most of these museums, incorporating slavery interpretation has brought a higher public profile and increases in audience and revenue. There are common elements to these success stories, including dedicated change-makers, committed leadership, and deliberate processes of reflection through techniques such as facilitated dialogue. Historical research can help drive the change process, and its public dissemination can jump-start public awareness. Developing new community partners can support and encourage transformation, building trust and lending authenticity to novel interpretations (see chapter 5, "The Necessity of Community Involvement: Talking about Slavery in the Twenty-First Century").

Historic house museums traditionally promote celebrity and prosperity, and the many northern enslaved people who lived in domestic spaces left comparatively few artifacts. Focusing on the glamour of the historic house and its material culture ignores comprehensive content; interpretation must actively counterbalance this. Comprehensive historic content provokes reactions. After all, enslavement is about treating people as commodities, which can provoke embarrassment, anger, discomfort, resentment, and fear. Yet the history of slavery, and responses to being enslaved, can also provoke pride, humility, inspiration, and understanding—powerful elements for organizational transformation and successful programs.

Notes

1. Peter Birkenhead, "Why We Still Can't Talk about Slavery," *Salon*, December 27, 2011. http://www.salon.com/2011/12/27/why_we_still_cant_talk_about_slavery/.

2. American Association for State and Local History, "Statement of Professional Standards and Ethics," updated June 2012. http://resource.aaslh.org/view/aaslh-statement-of-professional-standards-and-ethics/.
3. John Kotter, *Leading Change* (Boston: Harvard Business School Press, 1996); Candace Tangorra Matelic, "Understanding Change and Transformation in History Organizations," *History News* 63:2 (2008), 7–13.
4. Craig Steven Wilder, *Ebony & Ivy: Race, Slavery, and the Troubled History of America's Universities* (New York: Bloomsbury, 2013).
5. Anne Farrow, Joel Lang, and Jenifer Frank, *Complicity: How the North Promoted, Prolonged and Profited from Slavery* (New York: Ballantine, 2006).
6. Joanne Pope Melish, *Disowning Slavery: Gradual Emancipation and "Race" in New England, 1780–1860* (Ithaca, N.Y.: Cornell University Press, 1998).
7. Reach Advisors, "Museum Audience Insight," (blog). http://reachadvisors.typepad.com/.
8. "Strategic Plan," Mattatuckmuseum.org, 2014. https://www.mattatuckmuseum.org/ourmission.
9. Maxine Watts (Mattatuck Museum African American History Project and Committee) and Marie Galbraith (retired Mattatuck Museum executive director), interviews with the author.
10. Published as a children's book, with background notes and archival material: Marilyn Nelson, *Fortune's Bones: The Manumission Requiem* (Asheville, N.C.: Front Street, 2004).
11. Susan Dunne and Daniela Altimari, "A Slave Whose Bones Helped Train Doctors Gets a Proper Burial," *Los Angeles Times*, September 14, 2013.
12. Mattatuck Museum, "Strategic Plan 2014–2017," page 2. https://www.mattatuckmuseum.org/ourmission.
13. Ibid.
14. From the Linden Place website, www.lindenplace.org, as of June 1, 2014; Jim Connell (Linden Place, executive director) and Robin Tremblay (office manager) interviews with author.
15. The quotation is from http://www.tracingcenter.org/resources/background/james-dewolf/. For background, see, for example, Jay Coughtry, *The Notorious Triangle: Rhode Island and the African Slave Trade, 1700–1807* (Philadelphia: Temple University Press, 1981): "Without a doubt … the D'Wolfs had the largest interest in the African slave trade of any American family.… In the annals of the American slave trade, the D'Wolfs are without peer."
16. "Mission," Lindenplace.org, 2014. http://www.lindenplace.org/history.htm.
17. *Traces of the Trade: A Story from the Deep North*, directed by Katrina Browne (Boston: Ebb Pod Productions, 2008), DVD.
18. See www.tracingcenter.org; Thomas Norman DeWolf, *Inheriting the Trade: A Northern Family Confronts Its Legacy as the Largest Slave-Trading Dynasty in U.S. History* (Boston: Beacon, 2008); Thomas Norman DeWolf and Sharon Leslie Morgan, *Gather at the Table: The Healing Journey of a Daughter of Slavery and a Son of the Slave Trade* (Boston: Beacon, 2012); Cynthia Mestad Johnson, *James DeWolf and the Rhode Island Slave Trade* (Charleston, S.C.: History Press, 2014).
19. Linden Place, "Linden Place Museum News," Spring 2012, 4.
20. From the Royall House and Slave Quarters website, www.royallhouse.org, 2014. Tom Lincoln (executive director) and Gracelaw Simmons (board member) interviews with the author.
21. Wilder, *Ebony & Ivy*, 230.
22. Alexandra A. Chan, *Slavery in the Age of Reason: Archaeology at a New England Farm* (Knoxville: University of Tennessee Press, 2007), 1–3.
23. "Mission," Royallhouse.org, 2014. http://www.royallhouse.org/about-us/mission-board-and-staff/.

24. "Mission," harrietbeechersStowecenter.org, 2014. https://www.harrietbeecherstowecenter.org/about/index.shtml#mission.
25. Joseph Cialdella, "A Place of Collaboration: Cliveden and the Merits of Reevaluating a Landmark's Past," American Historical Association, *Perspectives on History* (December 2013).
26. David Young (Cliveden's executive director), interview with the author.
27. Cliveden Interpretive Plan, 2012.
28. Ibid.
29. Young, interview.
30. "Emancipating Cliveden," e-mail from Cliveden, June 29, 2012.
31. "A Year End Gift Is a Great Investment," e-mail from Cliveden, December 3, 2013.
32. Cialdella, "Place of Collaboration."

CHAPTER 5

The Necessity of Community Involvement

Talking about Slavery in the Twenty-First Century

DINA A. BAILEY AND RICHARD C. COOPER

> If [community involvement] policies are to be fully effective, it is vital that individuals and representatives from excluded and community groups are involved in developing, introducing and monitoring the service. Establishing and maintaining these links is time consuming, but every opportunity should be taken for fostering community consultation and partnership.
>
> —*COGS for Yorkshire Museum Council*[1]

UNTIL RECENTLY, community involvement with museums and historic sites was generally lacking and often hardly visible. Institutions kept tight control over their narratives, using archival documents and artifacts to support their interpretative choices. However, narratives become broader, deeper, and more inclusive when new perspectives are incorporated. As our circles of stakeholders have expanded, members of our communities have found (or have been allowed to find) their voices and are requesting inclusion in museum narratives. This, in turn, has enabled narratives to change, becoming more vibrant and authentic. We, as public historians and interpreters of history, now recognize that we are not in possession of the complete narrative—we need to involve the broader community within each of our institutions. One way of ensuring your institution's commitment to engaging communities is to write and implement a community involvement plan.

Background: Who Is Your Community?

Before creating a community involvement plan, institutions must think carefully about who composes their community. A community is made up of diverse groups of individual and institutional stakeholders, including educators, scholars, students, donors, neighbors, local government, colleges and universities, religious institutions, civic organizations, and businesses. At museums and historic sites that interpret slavery, community stakeholders may include descendants of the enslaved and slave owners, and other former residents of the site. Stakeholders can also be community members whose families' histories intersect with the history of slavery, whether or not their families were connected to the particular site. Some institutions may define their communities to include broader circles of stakeholders, including regional, state, or national governments, national nonprofit organizations, or even international partners. As professionals, we acknowledge that museums and historic sites do not create communities by themselves; rather, institutions have a responsibility to work with and within the communities in which they find themselves. It is important to build relationships that are both broad and deep—thus becoming active, collaborative participants in the presentation and discussion of complex, challenging topics with contemporary resonance, such as slavery.

When museums and historic sites interpret slavery, they open themselves up to remarkable opportunities for understanding the intricacies involved in telling a richer, more inclusive narrative. However, if an institution tries to control the entire story, the community will be less willing to engage with the story. Working with the community to create a pool of shared meaning or mutual understanding can ultimately drive commitment and the sustained involvement of a diverse group of people, helping to authentically communicate the historical narrative while actively participating in the present and ensuring a shared future.

In 2002, the American Association of Museums published a seminal work, *Mastering Civic Engagement: A Challenge to Museums*, as part of a new fieldwide initiative called "The Museums & Community Initiative." In this report, Ellen Hirzy challenged museums "to pursue their potential as active visible players in the community life," highlighting the necessity of making community involvement a shared process and not a "one-sided approach."[2] If museums intend only to meet their organization's needs, and not address the needs of the community, they risk losing the trust of those stakeholders. This is important to remember when building community involvement plans.

The Building Blocks of Best Practice

Developing a community involvement plan might seem daunting and overwhelming for many museums and historic sites, but we believe it's an essential component of best practices. In engaging our communities with the story of enslavement, there are multiple questions to consider:

- How do we responsibly build a diverse circle of storytellers within our community so that we hear and share previously unheard voices?

- How do we ensure that this diverse circle provides input into how we move forward, telling community stories with respect, dignity, and awareness with the result that *because* these stories include diverse perspectives, they are stronger and more valuable?
- How do we change the word "accountability" so that it doesn't have a negative connotation in this communal environment?
- And, perhaps most importantly, how do we broaden our understanding of our institution's place in the community?

With a community involvement plan, we can address these questions and strategically allow all voices to be heard. This plan is an essential part of interpreting a comprehensive history, with all of its complexities, and is important to fostering well-rounded, well-represented institutions. Although each plan is unique to an individual institution and its community, we want to provide some fundamental guidance to aid the planning process and to illustrate why community involvement plans are vital to sites seeking to interpret slavery. Here are five fundamental elements to consider when developing an effective community involvement plan.

1. **Create a supportive infrastructure:** Set clear community involvement goals, objectives, and policies for the institution. This ensures that the entire institution understands the purpose of community involvement and has a transparent framework for how the institution plans to engage the community at all levels of planning and operation.
2. **Engage a diversity of groups and individuals:** Partner with several different community groups and individuals. The range of voices at the table will lend credibility and support, especially when complex topics arise, and help ensure that your interpretation reflects a sufficiently wide range of perspectives. Institutions may consider looking for stakeholders outside of the local community, including historians, scholars, descendants, and other regional, national, or international partners.
3. **Listen to the needs of the community:** Listen attentively to the needs of the community, and ensure their voices are involved throughout the process. Set clear, realistic limits on the scope of the project, that is, do not overpromise on what the institution can deliver. In turn, the community needs to understand and accept its role and responsibilities to achieve agreed-upon goals.
4. **Create community forums:** Set up forums with members of the community to exchange knowledge so that all are heard and understood. These forums should take place both at the museum and at selected community sites. The intention of the forums should be clearly communicated with all involved and allow for constructive exchanges between the institution and community.
5. **Start with a specific project:** Community engagement requires dedicated staff time and institutional resources to forge effective partnerships. To ensure success, institutions should examine the community's needs, with input from the community, and select appropriate projects or topics that mutually benefit all involved. Start small, with one program, to gauge how institutional resources are allocated throughout the collaboration and monitor communication between you and your community partners.

These small steps help ameliorate the risk of endangering the respect and accountability of the institution caused by not being able to fully deliver on what is promised in the partnership. In creating a community involvement plan based on these five building blocks, it's important to remember that each plan should be unique to its institution. The following case studies highlight how organizations have developed and implemented plans that led to successful and sustained partnerships between the organization and the community.

Case Studies

Because community involvement plans are a relatively new institutional fixture, we've highlighted three case studies that reflect different approaches to welcoming the community into your institution. These case studies focus on telling complex stories of slavery that feature previously unheard voices.

Buxton National Historic Site and Museum

Buxton National Historic Site and Museum is located in a small community of about a hundred people in Buxton, Canada. The community historically known as the Elgin Settlement traces its roots to the nineteenth century and is one of four black settlements established

Figure 5.1. Descendants of former slaves, who sought freedom through the Underground Railroad to Canada, reunite for homecomings at Buxton National Historic Site and Museum in Ontario. Source: Buxton National Historic Site and Museum.

for those who fled enslavement in the United States. Extant on the site are numerous Underground Railroad resources, including a log cabin from 1850, a barn from 1853, and a church and cemetery from 1861. The institution's mission is to "collect, preserve, exhibit, and interpret historical artifacts related to the Elgin (Buxton) Settlement from its founding in 1849 to the late 19th century" and to "provide the personal histories and genealogies of the original settlers and their descendants through ongoing historical research."[3]

Buxton's immediate community is small, but the institution has succeeded by deliberately including local residents in the planning and execution of programs. This type of engagement is clearly stated in the institution's founding documents. Buxton's Community Standard Policy reads, "The Buxton Historical Society (BHS) recognizes their responsibility to make the museum collections accessible to the public, to actively involve the community, provide relative programming, and sponsor events that are open and responsive to the community."[4] This policy enables the institution to remain focused on the inclusion of the community within the overall strategic plan, purposely ensuring that the community is involved in their museum and making the organization aware that it is part of the larger community.

This community engagement policy is a large part of what drives sustainability at Buxton. Through sustained partnerships, individuals actively participate as storytellers, donors, and fundraisers, all seeing themselves as stewards of their community's legacy. Significant to this sustained partnership are the many descendants of the original black settlers of Buxton who reside in the area and continue to share family stories that have been passed down, and who tell personal stories of growing up with the responsibilities of this unique legacy. The respectful gathering and dissemination of this information gives the institution credibility and respect within the community and among nonlocal stakeholders (academics, museum professionals, and people of the wider African diaspora) across Canada and the United States.

The Buxton Museum develops opportunities for the community to actively participate in programs that focus on understanding the meaning of freedom. One example is their ongoing program "A Snapshot in the Family Album," which invites folks to share their family lineage through pictures, poems, skits, or song. Descendants use Buxton's collections, plus those at other repositories, to research their genealogy. So successful is the program that it continues to inspire others in the community to research their own family histories. The continuous building of family histories, which become part of the Buxton Museum collection, allows the institution to maintain community involvement throughout the year.

"Voices of Freedom," a program designed specifically for local students, centers around a 1910 photo taken in front of the site's 1861 schoolhouse. Each student takes on the persona of an individual in the photo, all of whom were the grandchildren of fugitive slaves and free people of color. The students research the lives of their assigned historical figures and examine "the road to freedom along which the grandparents of the 1910 students journey."[5] This program allows students to explore the challenges faced by multiple generations once freedom was obtained. This exchange between students and the stories of older generations of the community is replicable at many cultural institutions in the United States, whether the storyteller is a direct descendant or a witness who lived the history involved (e.g., participants in the civil rights movement).

Buxton takes community involvement to a greater extent with an annual celebration, the Buxton Homecoming, held since 1924. During Homecoming, this small, remote community is vibrant with descendants, family, friends, and others who return "home" to rekindle memories, renew a sense of kinship with their ancestors, and build new relationships. The event started as a one-day program and evolved into a four-day masterpiece, attracting nearly 3,000 people. (Total annual visitation at the site, not including Homecoming, is just under 6,000.) Residents of Buxton maintain active involvement in the programming and implementation of Homecoming. This consistent community support helps sustain the annual program and holds the Buxton Historical Society and the overall community jointly accountable for success. Shannon Prince, the museum's curator, confirms that "when the community is involved, it helps to 'build bridges' between museums and communities, [in order] to provide an opportunity for the people living in such communities to find out about their own heritage and to help them realize that it is through their active participation in museum activities that that heritage and rich legacy are kept alive."[6]

This institution focuses on life after slavery, and it is a unique celebration of people and stories. As museum professionals who interpret slavery, we must remember to celebrate agency and freedom. The awe of a simple freedom story ensnares an audience as much as staggering tales of enslavement. Most significant is the participation of descendants of the Elgin Settlement. They, more than any others, lend credibility to the institution and the stories that are shared, including stories gifted to visitors, who often travel hundreds of miles to participate in this celebration of freedom.

Somerset Place

Somerset Place, located approximately 30 miles outside of Plymouth, North Carolina, was one of the largest plantations in the upper South, encompassing approximately 100,000 acres. The site operated as an active plantation for eighty years, between 1785 and 1865. The original owner, Josiah Collins, imported 80 enslaved Africans, and during its active years, more than 850 enslaved people lived and worked on the plantation.

At the conclusion of the Civil War, the majority of those who had been enslaved moved away from the plantation, but those who stayed refused to work without pay. The Collins family abandoned the site in the early twentieth century, which led to vandalism and rapid deterioration. In the 1930s and 1940s, efforts increased to restore the site to its antebellum "glory." Local historic preservationists, the state of North Carolina, and, to some extent, the federal government, all participated in the restoration efforts. In 1969, the North Carolina Department of Cultural Resources designated Somerset Place as a state historic site.

Dorothy Spruill Redford, the author of *Somerset Homecoming: Recovering a Lost Heritage*, and Alisa Y. Harrison, who titled her PhD dissertation "Reconstructing Somerset Place: Slavery, Memory and Historical Consciousness," have revealed several factors that led to the failure of the early restoration efforts.[7] The restoration only highlighted the story of the plantation home and did not take into account the complex history of the large enslaved population that supported Somerset for eighty years. The site also primarily targeted a white audience. Although other sites may have had a similar format and target audience during this period in the 1930s and 1940s, the lack of a more complex story affected the success of this particular plantation. Many of the descendants of the enslaved still lived in the area and wanted to see themselves in the overall story of the site.

Figure 5.2. Students use early nineteenth-century techniques to make rope during a program at Somerset Place State Historic Site. Enslaved people on the plantation made rope, which was sold to local shipbuilders and used on the plantation.
Source: Somerset Place State Historic Site.

The site's positive transition began with the 1977 airing of the television mini-series *Roots*. The show, and the book it was based on, led to an increased recognition of, and appreciation for, African American history, especially during the period of enslavement, and it encouraged many African Americans to actively research their own family histories through oral histories and genealogical research. Through her own *Roots*-inspired genealogical research, Dorothy Spruill Redford discovered she was a descendant of one of the original enslaved Africans brought to Somerset Place. Because of this discovery, Redford began to frequent the plantation. Her repeated visits led the site manager to ask her to make a presentation to visitors coming to the site. Through being open to Redford sharing her story at the site, the organization began the process of accepting a new story into its narrative and providing a path for her voice to play a role as the organization moved forward.

On the day of the presentation, Redford stationed herself in the kitchen, but many of the visitors passed right by her and the kitchen all together. She recognized a pattern that needed to change at Somerset Place. Redford developed what she called "homecomings" to bring descendants of plantation residents back to Somerset, hoping they would become engaged with the site. She traveled around the community, knocking on doors, sending letters, handing out flyers, and visiting churches, all the while encouraging African American community members to visit the plantation and become part of the storytelling experience. Her grassroots community initiative paid off. Between 1986 and 2001, these homecomings brought more than 5,000 visitors from across the United States to the plantation.

The homecomings began a period of active and sustained community involvement at Somerset Place. Descendants, in particular, continue to support the site as ambassadors, donors, volunteers, researchers, and interpreters. This site is unusual in that a single, determined community member, not on staff, took the lead to rally community involvement with the site. It is important to remember that sometimes institutions have to allow the community to be a driving force behind transition and innovation.

The National Underground Railroad Freedom Center

The National Underground Railroad Freedom Center in Cincinnati, Ohio, opened its doors in 2004. The Freedom Center's vision is to inspire and empower a growing force of freedom-seekers and modern-day "freedom conductors," that is, those who fight for the rights of others, respect human dignity, engage in honest and open dialogue, and act with courage to support the long journey to freedom for all people. With examples from the era of the Underground Railroad experience (antebellum history) to modern-day freedom struggles, the Freedom Center brings to life heroic stories of courage, cooperation, and perseverance in the pursuit of freedom. Using the fundamental human need for freedom from enslavement as a common ground, the Freedom Center provides forums that are inclusive for dialogue and encourages every individual to take a journey that advances freedom and personal growth.

The Freedom Center developed a comprehensive community involvement plan that enables the institution to work closely with not only the local community but also the national and international communities. The plan was born when the institution realized that to remain credible, relevant, and engaging to the overall community it must find and

Figure 5.3. Visitors explore the "From Slavery to Freedom" gallery at the National Underground Railroad Freedom Center, which portrays three centuries of slavery, from its introduction in the colonies to its abolition at the end of the Civil War.
Source: National Underground Railroad Freedom Center.

develop connections between historic slavery and modern-day issues. The institution did this by placing contemporary human trafficking in the continuum of the history of slavery, which helps to drive a deeper understanding of the true nature of slavery over time and the vigilance required to end it. This linking of historical and modern-day slavery has significantly grown the Freedom Center's impact within, and accountability to, the global community. With this expanded role interpreting contemporary slavery, the Freedom Center has broadened its definition of community to include a wider range of stakeholders. Bringing a wide range of communities to the table breathed new life into the institution, and now stakeholders, local, national, and international, are coming to the Freedom Center with partnership ideas, instead of the Center having to seek them out.

In 2012, the Freedom Center entered into a cooperative grant agreement with the US Department of State's Office to Monitor and Combat Trafficking in Persons to produce a global antislavery campaign. The campaign used stories of ten modern antislavery "heroes" honored in the Department's 2012 *Trafficking in Persons Report* to encourage antislavery collaborations between the US government and foreign nations. The campaign involved events in roughly fifty nations over nine months, featuring the Freedom Center documentary *Journey to Freedom*, a poster, and a series of brochures that introduced the topic to a global audience.[8] This partnership has continued with annual visits to the Freedom Center by each class of *Trafficking in Persons Report* heroes and with ongoing projects aimed at telling their inspirational stories through Freedom Center exhibits and its website.

The Freedom Center also maintains a direct partnership with several leading antitrafficking nongovernmental organizations (NGOs), including Polaris Project, Free the Slaves, GoodWeave, and International Justice Mission. These community partners all contributed content to the Freedom Center's permanent exhibition *Invisible: Slavery Today*, developed in 2010, and are part of discussions to update the exhibit moving forward.

At the local level, the Freedom Center partnered with community groups and local universities to create the Teaching for Hope & Justice Network. This network is a grassroots movement committed to providing space for social justice and humanities education through professional development workshops. The workshops were developed by and for K–12 teachers and students, preservice teachers (college students preparing to become teachers), the local community, and teacher educators. Since 2011, these workshops have reached over 1,000 participants.

The Freedom Center's link of historical and modern issues enables the institution to successfully engage with the community at home and abroad. The community partners provide credibility to the institution along with new content and stories that enhance its interpretation. The Freedom Center's willingness to open its doors and allow the community to actively engage with the institution expands the reach of the institution far beyond its walls.

Applying Best Practices

Best practices for the interpretation of slavery require that institutions make community involvement essential to their operations. The better the community involvement plan and the effectiveness of its implementation, the more effective and relevant an institution is likely to be. Certainly, plans must be unique to each institution and each community, but the basic elements of community involvement remain the same. These elements include bringing more diverse voices to the table, developing plans to retain these voices and community input into the future, having the institution and the community hold each other accountable in positive and constructive ways, and recognizing the institution's unique role in the broader community. Institutions must always keep best practices at the center of their strategic planning. The field has a responsibility to be consistent in our efforts to involve the community. Slavery is a complex and challenging topic, and people are often sensitive about the brutality of enslavement and the difficulties of freedom, shying away from what is not familiar. However, a solid community involvement plan, and a determination not to dismiss the needs of either the institution or the community, ensures a comprehensive and conscientious interpretation of slavery.

Notes

1. COGS for Yorkshire Museum Council, *Community Involvement for Museums, Archives and Libraries: Toolkit for Improving Practice* (Sheffield, UK: COGS, 2002), 1.
2. Ellen Hirzy, "Mastering Civic Engagement: A Report from the American Association of Museums," in *Mastering Civic Engagement: A Challenge to Museums* (Washington, D.C.: American Association of Museums Press, 2002), 9.
3. Buxton Museum, "Statement of Purpose," last updated April 2012. http://www.buxton museum.com/mandates/purpose.html.
4. Buxton Museum, "Community Standard Policy," last updated May 2013. http://buxtonmuseum .com/mandates/community.html.
5. Buxton Museum, "The Learning Centre: Voices of Freedom," last updated April 2014. http:// www.buxtonmuseum.com/education/ed-vof.html.
6. Shannon Prince, e-mail message to the authors, October 2, 2013.
7. Dorothy Spruill Redford, with Michael D'Orso, *Somerset Homecoming: Recovering a Lost Heritage* (Chapel Hill: University of North Carolina Press, 1988); Alisa Y. Harrison, "Reconstructing Somerset Place: Slavery, Memory and Historical Consciousness" (PhD dissertation, Duke University, 2008).
8. *Journey to Freedom* can be viewed on the Freedom Center website. http://freedomcenter.org/ enabling-freedom/journey-to-freedom.

CHAPTER 6

Visitors Are Ready, Are We?

CONNY GRAFT

ARE VISITORS interested in learning about slavery and the lives of enslaved people at historic sites and museums? When exposed to the difficult and painful stories of enslaved people, what are visitors' reactions? What have we learned from visitor studies on this topic and how can we use the lessons learned to strengthen exhibits and interpretive programs dealing with slavery?

In this chapter, I explore these and related questions to help historic sites and museums think intentionally about how they can construct honest and informative interpretations about this complex and significant part of our nation's history.

Finding historic sites and museums that include the history of slavery and the story of the enslaved as a major part of their interpretation is a challenge. Finding sites which do that *and* have visitors evaluate their work is a bigger challenge. Many sites and museums have limited resources, but there are plenty of examples of small museums that manage to conduct useful evaluations on a variety of topics.[1] The studies I discuss in this chapter focus on different aspects of the experience of slavery and different types of presentation methods. They all use different methods to evaluate the experience of visitors. One limitation of these evaluations is that they focus only on current visitors, not on potential visitors. Despite this, these studies offer lessons that can help sites and museums understand how visitors think about slavery and how they react to its interpretation.

Feedback from Visitor Surveys

Expectations about the Role of Museums and Controversial Topics

Before looking at studies focused on visitor expectations regarding slavery, it is useful to acknowledge broader studies that investigate visitors' expectations regarding controversial topics. One such important study, "Exhibitions as Contested Sites: The Roles of Museums in Contemporary Society," was conducted by the Australian Research Council between 2001 and 2003, with input from the University of Sydney, several Australian museums, and the Canadian Museums Association.[2] Museum audiences in Australia and Canada were asked to reflect on the roles museums could play in contemporary society. The study also sought to determine how museums can effectively mount exhibitions on controversial topics. The study's methodology included telephone interviews of both museum and nonmuseum goers in Australia; exit surveys at the Australian Museum, the Australian War Memorial, and at three Canadian museums; focus groups with museum visitors in Australia; and an online survey with museum staff and stakeholders in the United States, the United Kingdom, Australia, New Zealand, and Canada. The controversial topics, named by the people participating in the interviews and focus groups, included indigenous issues, immigration, population levels, asylum seekers, death, terrorism, treatment of prisoners of war, war atrocities, drugs, sex, religion, racism, social justice, globalization, sustainability of the environment, and genetic engineering. This study explored many aspects of how respondents felt about the role of museums in presenting such controversial topics.

The study found that more than half of survey respondents in Canada and Australia felt that museums do have a role in presenting controversial topics. Comments included:

> "If museums don't do it, who will?"
>
> "Museums are a public forum for issues that should challenge society."
>
> "Hiding something doesn't help kids and the future of Canada. You have to air it in order to get to the truth, whatever the truth is."[3]

Respondents also felt strongly that museums should allow visitors to make comments about controversial topics. Participants wanted museums to provide opportunities for visitors to have a say through feedback forms, suggestion boxes, tours, lectures or seminars, and discussion groups with guest speakers, with the ability to opt out. Between 70 and 80 percent of respondents in the United States, United Kingdom, Australia, New Zealand, and Canada view museums as places for challenging people's ways of thinking. In this context, "challenging" means providing an honest, uncensored picture of an issue, with multiple viewpoints and scholarly information based on sound research.

Another example of museums challenging people's way of thinking and addressing challenging contemporary social issues is the National Dialogues on Immigration project, which is part of the International Coalition of Sites of Conscience. Between 2010 and 2013, twenty leading history museums and cultural centers across the United States held local public dialogues on immigration in seventeen cities and thirteen states, from Georgia to Washington State. Employing innovative facilitated dialogue tools, participating sites engaged nearby communities in discussions about US immigration from past to present. Sites include former historic immigration stations; places that highlight immigrant stories; civil rights, human rights, and social justice institutions; sites near borderlands addressing issues of belonging and exclusion; and sites that raise questions about regional and national identity as a way to address increasing diversity in their communities. Some dialogues connect to a featured exhibition, and others are using community dialogues to create exhibitions. The sites doing this work are finding that attracting visitors to participate in dialogues about a challenging subject has not been an issue. In addition, participants' evaluations placed a high value on having the opportunity to come together to discuss immigration issues past and present. For example, 95 percent of the visitors who participated in dialogues in the southeastern United States stated the dialogue programs were very valuable, and 88 percent of visitors in the Southwest stated the dialogue programs were very valuable. In exit surveys, 75 to 86 percent of the people who participated in the dialogues in both regions stated that the dialogue, convened at museums and historic sites, helped them to see immigration from a different perspective.[4]

Both of these studies provide evidence that audiences want to be challenged and expect museums to bring people together to discuss controversial and sensitive topics. To do this, sites must make dialogue and discussion a key part of their interpretation. If this means sacrificing some thematic interpretive objectives to provide time and space for dialogue, this is a sacrifice that visitors will support. One of my favorite sayings, when reviewing a list of outcome statements and interpretive themes with historic sites, is "Take your list, cut this list in half, divide the number of outcomes and themes by three, and then do it again." Creating exhibits that pose questions and give visitors space to share opinions with each other, and the museum, via sticky notes, drawings, or video recordings will leave a more meaningful and memorable impression on visitors.

So, does this mean that there are historic site and museum visitors who expect to be challenged and presented with the topic of slavery? What evidence do we have, if any, that this is true? What other factors impact visitors' expectations about this topic?

Impact of Racial Identity on Visitor Expectations

One of the most thorough studies of visitor expectations about slavery was conducted by the African Burial Ground National Monument in New York City.[5] This site is the earliest known African and African American cemetery in the United States, in use from the 1600s to the 1790s. More than 15,000 men, women, and children are buried there. The cemetery was rediscovered in 1999 during excavation for the construction of a federal government building.

In preparation for the design and construction of a national monument to mark the cemetery, front-end and formative evaluations were conducted by Jeff Hayward of the firm People, Places and Design. For the front-end evaluation, visitors were interviewed in nine different museums throughout the city. It is important to note that the purpose of this study was not to determine what stories the African Burial Ground site would tell or how they would tell them. The purpose was to discover which topics and experiences interest visitors so they could be used as hooks to entice people to visit the site. The key findings show a diversity of expectations influenced by the interviewee's current understanding of the historical narrative and by their racial identity.

When asked about their level of interest, 80 percent of African Americans indicated a high interest in both the site and its story, and 40 percent of those who were not African American indicated a high interest in visiting the site (~80%) and in African American history (~82%). Of non–African American survey participants, 45 percent had a high interest in visiting the site and only 16 percent rated as highly interested in African American

Figure 6.1. The stories of the African Burial Ground teach visitors how free and enslaved Africans contributed to Lower Manhattan during the seventeenth and eighteenth centuries.
Source: National Park Service.

history.[6] The non–African American respondents were more interested in how the history of the site would expand their knowledge of New York City and colonial history in general. In a follow-up formative study, visitors to two different museums in New York City were shown prototypes of the exhibits for the African Burial Ground site and asked to share their reactions to the exhibits. Many people anticipated having a heightened emotional response to the exhibits as they thought about racism and the horrors of slavery. Although all groups shared an anticipation of unpleasant reactions, people of African descent said they were also likely to feel pride and inspiration.

Another example of the impact of racial identity on expectations is a front-end study conducted by the National Museum of African American History and Culture in Washington, D.C. The study asked respondents to talk about their perceptions of the phrase "African American history and culture." Non–African Americans were most likely to mention art, music, and entertainment when thinking about African American history and culture. They also mentioned slavery, the Civil War, and well-known individuals. African Americans were most likely to mention the contributions, successes, and achievements of African Americans, lesser known people and events, and positive attributes of African American culture, such as strength, pride, and perseverance.[7]

A fundamental lesson from these two studies is that racial identity has a large effect on visitor expectations and experiences. Note that only African Americans talked about pride and inspiration as a desired outcome in both studies. Isn't instilling pride and inspiration an outcome that all museums should inspire to? We may be understandably wary about negative and emotional reactions to the stories of enslaved people, but how many museums have thought about positive outcomes such as pride and inspiration? By deemphasizing the stories of enslaved people, have museums unintentionally missed opportunities to help Americans recognize and honor the courage and spirit of enslaved people and to foster feelings of pride and inspiration about this history?

Given this research on the import of racial identity on visitor expectations, how can we use that information to develop responsible and meaningful experiences for current and potential visitors? It is critical that audiences (current and potential) from diverse racial and ethnic backgrounds become involved in the process of planning these programs. This can be done via a front-end study, such as the one conducted at the African Burial Ground. It can also be done by convening listening sessions (informal meetings for soliciting responses to focused questions) with community groups that include people with diverse racial and ethnic identities to hear about the proposed project and then share their own expectations of the experience.[8] Another approach is to recruit African Americans in the communities surrounding the museum to become advisors and partners in the planning of exhibits and programs. A good example of this type of collaboration is described in an article about the development of the former Transatlantic Gallery (now the International Slavery Museum) at the Merseyside Maritime Museum in Liverpool, England.[9] The museum conducted conversations with the black public in Liverpool throughout the entire planning process, and this revealed important expectations and insights that informed critical decisions about the content, tone, and techniques used in their exhibits and programs. This approach also provided support for and a sense of ownership in the exhibit.

Preconceived Narratives and Meaning-Making

As described in Lois Silverman's article "Commentary: Reflections on the Adolescence of Meaning-Making," visitors make multiple meanings of the interpretations they experience regardless of the topic. Many of the meanings visitors make are not ones that we, as professionals, are in control of. As Silverman writes, "visitors [are] alongside staff as active, equal partners in the construction of exhibition meanings."[10]

Given that people make their own meanings of a museum's narrative, museums should be aware of the factors that influence visitors' meaning-making. A major factor is the historical narrative people bring with them to the visiting experience. As other heritage tourism studies have shown, visitors are not blank slates. By choosing to visit a particular historic site, visitors "partake in an experience that often becomes a continuation of their psycho-social selves. It therefore follows that individuals, be they dominant or resistant publics, construct meanings that serve as a foundation on which to base their identities."[11]

Visitors are exposed to a variety of popular texts, such as movies, novels, websites, and books, in addition to family stories handed down through generations, about the institution of slavery. Christine N. Buzinde and Carla Almeida Santos conducted a study at the Hampton Plantation State Historic Site in McClellanville, South Carolina, that revealed this bias. Recognizing that visitors arrive with preconstructed narratives, Buzinde and Santos interviewed visitors to uncover how they react to interpretations of slavery that may be similar or dissimilar to the historical narrative they arrived with. They conducted twenty-seven on-site exit interviews in February 2006, asking visitors:

"What does this site represent to you?"

"What significance does it possess?"

"Why should it be commemorated?"

"Are there other elements that should be added to the overall narrative? If so, what are they, and in what ways would these additions be beneficial?"[12]

Although the study did not include an observation of the tour taken by visitors, the responses show how visitors can walk away with opposing impressions of how enslaved people were treated at this particular site. Two overarching themes emerged from the survey responses: "Slavery as a Munificent Institution" and "Slavery as a Lesson for Humanity." Some visitors accepted the interpretation they heard at the site, others refused to accept the same narrative. The visitors' responses show how their reactions depended upon meanings they constructed about the topic before they toured the site.

The visitors who walked away with the idea that slavery was a munificent institution and that the masters were altruistic toward their slaves offered comments like these:

But people were well here because I read books that stated that [an enslaved person] wanted to be a Rutledge servant as opposed to someone else. I mean some of them were mean to their slaves . . . but they didn't do that here. Some days they showed up for work some days they didn't, and it was okay.

From what we heard Archibald's ancestors were nice folk . . . they were good to their servants, they tried to treat them well. Did y'all see the cemetery at the entrance, they gave up the huge property . . . gave it to their workers so they could all be buried there. Nice people like that were hard to come by in those days . . . and Archie writes a lot about Sue [a former slave] 'nd how nice she was.

Conversely, other visitors who heard the same narrative on the tour emphasized that Hampton Plantation's slaves were *not* treated well and that this story provides an important lesson:

I felt that the treatment of the enormous riches that were gotten through slavery was not treated as forcefully or strongly as I would hope it [to] be.

It doesn't matter how well slaves were "well treated" it doesn't alter the fact that they were slaves. It's morally repulsive. [It's] a beautiful plantation but founded on an immoral concept. I think you just have to try and present it honestly.

I would have liked to see more about the slaves and their enslavers . . . [the lack of focus on the institution of slavery] explains a lot of things in terms of current attitudes and what the relationships are . . . these kinds of places should help people reflect upon the past and then address the current economic and social inequities because they are valuable.

This study shows that the interpretation at Hampton Plantation is just one of many factors that influence meanings that visitors make: "They constructed their own meanings of the plantation through discursive strategies of presencing/absencing and, as such, endorsed certain discourses while disenfranchising the possibility of others."[13] Hampton Plantation staff updated the training manual in response to the study, but they did not have the resources to follow up by taking other steps, including a planned online survey.

If Hampton Plantation had been able to do so, reflecting on the results of this study and assessing the state of the current interpretation might have afforded them the opportunity to make changes to their mission, strategic plan, and interpretive themes and techniques. This would have let them better serve their visitors by providing a more comprehensive and conscientious narrative of slavery based on insights into how prior knowledge affects the meanings visitors make of their experience. Visitors whose "psycho-social selves" have led them to internalize narratives about the munificence of slavery, for instance, might benefit from being exposed to supplementary material on the daily lives of the enslaved, to additional stories or perspectives to aid the gradual process of wrestling with this new knowledge about slavery, or even the chance to engage in dialogue with the interpreter or other visitors.

Understanding how a site's interpretation agrees with or disagrees with a visitor's world view is just as important as whether they enjoyed the visit. Museums can learn more about the historical narratives that visitors bring with them by conducting a formal front-end study. It is important to encourage visitors to share their narratives as a part of a dialogue, either at the beginning of a tour or program or throughout the interpretation. Providing visitors a chance to discuss their thoughts about the interpretation allows them to more easily process the conflicting narratives in their heads. This helps them to connect and associate information so that it will be absorbed and remembered, instead of being pushing aside.[14] Interpretation that focuses on helping visitors understand how their current and new narratives about slavery relate to one another will help to "lure diverse populations and facilitate wider voice resonance within depictions."[15]

Visitor Resistance to New Narratives

The studies included in this chapter provide evidence of visitor resistance to interpretations of slavery. Understanding why visitors may be resistant can help museums think about how to respond. In studying resistance to difficult knowledge and thinking about ways to help museum staff overcome their own resistance, Julia Rose, executive director of West Baton Rouge Museum in Port Allen, Louisiana, developed a set of strategies she refers to as "Commemorative Museum Pedagogy."[16] This approach, based on Freudian psychology, focuses on techniques for interpreting the stories of oppressed groups, and Rose's descriptions of the cognitive and psychological reactions people have to these stories help explain the diversity of reactions that visitors have to interpretive experiences in museums and historic sites. Similarly, Kristin Gallas and James Perry have drawn on new scholarship into the role played by historical narratives in identity, exploring the cognitive and affective responses people exhibit in response to interpretations of slavery, or other traditionally marginalized history, that challenge narratives at the core of their identities (see chapter 1, "Comprehensive Content and Contested Historical Narratives").

When visitors question information, ask for more evidence that supports the information, or even dispute the information they are receiving, this does not always mean that they are truly denying that something happened. They may be trying to process and come to terms with stories they have never been exposed to. And those seemingly negative reactions may actually be a positive sign that they are beginning to reconsider what they once knew.

The dissonance that occurs internally when people are faced with novel information is exemplified by an exit interview conducted at Colonial Williamsburg following a dramatic interpretation called "Affairs of the Heart." In the program, first-person interpreters reenact a story about a master who had an affair with one of his slaves, fathering a mulatto child. After it is announced that he is marrying a white woman, he tells his slave-mistress that when they move to their new home he wants to take his mulatto son. A very emotional dialogue follows. In the exit interview, an African American woman stated that she was forced to come to Colonial Williamsburg by her employer. She said she would never have come otherwise, because she did not believe that there was anything at this site for her. She was moved by the program, but she was not sure she could believe what she was seeing or hearing. She said that it was very hard for her to imagine something like this actually happening, but she was willing to think that it might be possible this happened. Though not all visitors will be able to articulate their internal struggles, and be as openly receptive to new knowledge as this visitor was, similar experiences are likely to be motivating many of the outwardly less positive reactions of visitors to interpretation that challenges them, cognitively and emotionally.

Influence of Immersive Experiences on Visitors

When visiting historic sites, guests describe their desire to "feel like I am back then." Their expectation is that they will be immersed in the past. Historic sites use many different methods to achieve this outcome, one of which is total immersion in the environment, in the role of a particular person. One of the most successful immersion programs is "Follow the North Star" at Conner Prairie Interactive History Park in Fishers, Indiana. In fact, immersion is one of the main goals of the program.[17] This special program is only offered at night. Years of research, consultations with historians, conversations with members of the African American community, and prototyping went into the design and implementation of this program. Since 1999, more than 60,000 people have participated.

During the program, guests become fugitive slaves running from slave hunters, fleeing from captivity and risking everything for freedom. The brutal reality of being a fugitive slave is not spared, as author Carl Weinberg describes:

> I am standing in the woods. . . . A tall figure, whose face I cannot see, approaches. "What kind of work have you done, boy?" he asks. I say nothing, embarrassed that I have no identifiable trade, no definite skill like blacksmithing. "I don't know nothing about no irons," I stammer. He pauses, then asks, menacingly, "Are you a nancy boy?" "No, sir," I answer. "Are you a nancy boy?" he asks again. "No, sir," I repeat. "Get over there with

Figure 6.2. Guests assume the roles of freedom-seekers on the Underground Railroad, fleeing from enslavement and risking everything for freedom. "Follow the North Star" plays out as an intense, living drama where guests become actors on a 200-acre stage, running from slave hunters and working together to navigate the Underground Railroad to freedom.
Source: "Follow the North Star" program, Conner Prairie Interactive History Park.

> those breeders!" he commands. I comply and move from the line of "bucks" to join the "breeders."[18]

Participants recounted their emotional experiences of the program:[19]

> The experience was interesting. It made you think, to say the least ... you can expect to be degraded, to get dirty and to get mad. The similarities between the injustices and inequality found in 1836 are eerily similar to behaviors we notice today. It seemed not unlike some of the racial profiling we see today. Kudos [to] Conner Prairie for sparking these thoughts and using the arts to delve into such a tough subject.

> When my brother was laid on the ground, I thought about what it would be like watching my family get hurt.

> The fear I experienced in only 2 hours. I can't imagine having to endure that every day for 14 years.

What can the field learn from our colleagues who have implemented this type of immersive experience? Reading through hundreds of comments shared by participants, several key factors emerge that contributed to visitors' powerful reactions. First and foremost is engagement of all the senses. As educators we know the power of multisensory experiences, and here is one of the best examples of this. Words respondents used to describe their reactions include descriptions of sights, sounds, kinesthetic actions, smells, and taste: "slave yelling," "the cold," "getting on knees," "laying on stomach with face in dirt," "the moist cornbread," "the candle on the window," "the gunshots in the darkness," "the smell of wood," "the smell of the dirt," and "the darkness."[20]

The visitor comments, when compared to comments from other studies, are especially rich and powerful. Part of this has to do with the immersion factor and the use of drama that builds anticipation while also introducing ambiguity. One other factor that helps us understand the depth of meanings and memories people constructed from this experience is that the feedback was not collected on-site right after the program but via online surveys. Participants shared their reactions after they had time to return to their present world, reflect on what happened, talk with others about the experience, and unpack how the experience affected them. Collecting feedback from visitors with online surveys often reveals more thoughtful and honest feedback.

Participant feedback has been used to shape the program during the many years it has been running. For example, several years ago, the slave-catcher character, Ben Cannon, was dropped from the public program (kept in the school program) after a couple of incidents of participants physically challenging the interpreter/actor playing him. This was a hard decision and received some criticism, but the occasional incidents were a safety concern and distracted from the group's experience as seen in visitor comments on an online survey. It also allowed the staff to enhance the African American perspective by adding a former slave character, who is trying to go south to free his wife and son. As the director of interpretation for Conner Prairie stated, "It's always a balancing act between intensity and safety. We never want to incite extreme behavior, but the experience has to be intense to feel at all real. If not, it does not serve the subject of slavery."[21]

For museums and historic sites that do not employ living history or role-playing, this type of program may seem beyond their reach. Sites need to ask themselves: Is this type of program right for our site? Is the content appropriate? Do we have the resources to make it happen? Does it support our mission? Within your community there may be theater groups, performing arts organizations, historians at nearby universities, and members of the African American community who would be interested in helping create immersive experiences. Working with others to provide meaningful experiences focused on the lives of people who were enslaved can also help build important bridges between and among institutions and community groups that might not otherwise work together.

Best Practices: Incorporating Visitor Feedback into Your Interpretation

Given the lessons learned from the evaluations, here are some suggestions for consideration at your institution.

1. Acknowledge that visitors are ready to learn and participate in honest discussions of uncensored stories about slavery and people who were enslaved. Stories that are based on sound research and include multiple points of view can make a big impact.
2. Acknowledge the challenges and fears visitors face when confronting slavery. Have empathy with those who are resistant to hearing about slavery. Work with experienced facilitators who are trained in this history and its implications in order to help staff practice facilitating discussions about slavery and the legacies of this controversial part of our nation's history.
3. Involve people of different races and ethnicities in creating programs and exhibits. Do not wait until all the plans have been signed and sealed. Listen to what people have to say, and think about how best to provide multiple points of view. Consider working with performing arts organizations, artists, and theater groups to provide dramatic and immersive experiences.
4. Consider beginning with the present. Contact experts in contemporary issues, such as racism, prejudice, and inequality, and those who can help connect the dots between past and present. Invite them as partners to help you and your staff understand critical issues your community faces today related to inequality and how contemporary tensions and challenges arise out of our shared past. Knowing how the legacies of slavery impact our lives today can help us understand the narratives our visitors bring with them to our sites.
5. Provide time and space for visitors to share their own knowledge, experiences, and reactions within the exhibit and during the interpretive experience. Allow for dialogue between visitors and staff and among visitors themselves. Create feedback areas in your exhibit or welcome center for visitors to write, draw, or otherwise express their thoughts about the experience.

Tips for Planning and Implementing Evaluations

Making evaluations a part of institutional culture is critical to learning what we can about our visitors and incorporating that into the development of our interpretations.

1. Be intentional. Think about what you want visitors to think about, feel, and do, both during and after the experience. Share your ideas with your target audiences to investigate the outcomes they want from the experience. Revise your outcomes as you continue to gather feedback and suggestions.
2. Be nimble and experiment. Start with a small project and use evaluations as a tool to plan that experience. Lessons learned from just one project can be applied to many other experiences at your institution. Look at the case studies in *The Small Museum Toolkit* to see how this can be done with limited resources.[22] Use the resources of the American Association for State and Local History, such as their Visitors Count program, StEPs program, and Visitors' Voices affinity group, to learn how to conduct evaluations.
3. Build evaluations into your budgets when applying for grants. Many government agencies and foundations require that you devote part of their funding to evaluations, and others will likely appreciate your interest in doing so.

4. Consider collecting feedback from visitors with online surveys to gather more honest and meaningful comments. Collect e-mail addresses on-site and ask visitors if they would like to provide comments on their experience or be part of a VIP advisory group helping your site develop an exhibit or program on slavery. Visitors want to be involved and are often delighted to be asked to help.
5. Publish your findings and share what you have learned at conferences. Consider sharing your studies on www.informalscience.org. This site contains one of the largest online databases of evaluation studies conducted in all types of museums, parks, zoos, and botanical gardens.
6. Document how your study was conducted, any lessons learned, and how you used them to improve the visitor experience. If changes were not made, document this and explain why. This is critically important. When researching this chapter, I found that at several sites, current staff either did not know about a study conducted by their predecessors or had no record of how the study was used.

There are visitors who are ready to be challenged and to talk with each other about the meanings they make from the stories of enslaved people. They are also ready to talk about the legacy of slavery. Those not ready still need to be exposed to the stories of enslaved people. Museums can provide a safe place for people to come together and talk. It is my hope that this chapter will inspire historic sites and museums to use evaluations to develop honest interpretations of slavery and the lives of enslaved people, and to make this a core part of the visitor experience. Now it is our turn to get ready, to be intentional about our outcomes, think evaluatively, connect contemporary issues with the past, collect feedback before, during, and after the experience, and, most importantly, share what we have learned. As I stated in the beginning of this chapter, I could not find many history organizations that are actually interpreting slavery as a core part of their program *and* are evaluating the experience. We cannot afford to wait any longer. Make a commitment to do this and share your evaluation findings. We can do this.

Notes

1. Conny Graft and Stacy Klingler, "Reaching and Responding to the Audience," in *The Small Museum Toolkit*, eds. Cinnamon Catlin-Legutko and Stacy Klingler (Maryland: Altamira, 2011), 1022–2029 .
2. Linda Kelley, "Measuring the Impact of Museums on Their Communities: The Role of the 21st Century Museum" (paper presented at the International Council of Museums, 2006).
3. Ibid.
4. Conny Graft, "2013 Evaluation Report for the International Coalition of Sites of Conscience" (unpublished report, 2013), 9.
5. National Park Service. Jeff Hayward and Brian Werner, "Analysis of Potential Audiences for the African Burial Ground," 1–30. http://www.nps.gov/hfc/services/evaluation/ (accessed June 2014).
6. Ibid., 2.

7. Rex Ellis, e-mail message to author, December 9, 2013.
8. Janeen Bryant and Kamille Bostick, "What's the Big Idea? Using Listening Sessions to Build Relationships and Relevance," *History News*, Technical Leaflet #268 (Summer 2013), 1–8.
9. Anthony Tibbles, "Transatlantic Slavery: Against Human Dignity" (paper presented at the interim meeting of the International Congress of Maritime Museums, Curacao, October 2001).
10. H. Lois Silverman, "Commentary: Reflections on the Adolescence of Meaning-Making," *Exhibitionist* (Spring 2013), 61.
11. Christine N. Buzinde and Carla Almeida Santos, "Interpreting Slavery Tourism," *Annals of Tourism Research* 36:3 (2009), 439–58.
12. Ibid., 445.
13. Ibid.
14. John Medina, *Brain Rules: 12 Principles for Surviving and Thriving at Work, Home, and School* (Seattle: Pear, 2009), 121.
15. Buzinde and Santos, "Interpreting Slavery Tourism."
16. Ibid., 18.
17. Catherine Hughes, e-mail to author, June 2, 2014.
18 Weinberg, "Discomfort Zone."
19. Ibid.
20. Ibid.
21. Ibid.
22. Catlin-Legutko and Klingler, *Small Museum Toolkit.*

CHAPTER 7

Developing Competent and Confident Interpreters

PATRICIA BROOKS

"AREN'T YOU glad your ancestors were brought here as slaves so you don't have to live in Africa?" "Weren't slaves cared for and fed by their masters? So, really they were just working for room and board."

I have faced these questions many times as an interpreter of African American history. How do you prepare interpreters to address such questions? How can you equip them to peel away the layers of meaning represented in these questions—from the idea that ultimately slavery was beneficial, to the assumption that life in Africa would be a nightmare—and help a visitor grasp the historical complexities of slavery? As more historic sites and museums recognize their responsibility to interpret the history of slavery, they are faced with the challenge of successfully training staff to handle a story that engenders deep emotions for both museum employees and their visiting public. This task is not as arduous or alien as you might fear. Training interpreters to discuss slavery involves teaching skills and concepts that are common in training for all interpretation, but they may require reconceptualization of some elements. This chapter outlines four elements to consider when training third person interpreters to handle the subject of slavery: (1) redefining successful training goals and expectations; (2) reexamining the role that interpreters play in supporting a visitor's process of grappling with difficult knowledge; (3) considering language with purpose; and (4) using primary sources and material cultural to introduce multiple perspectives.

Redefining Successful Training

Training always begins with setting clear objectives. What skills and knowledge do you want interpreters to develop during the training process? Trainers usually aim for interpreters to be comfortable with the materials and skills presented during the training course. Conversely, when training on the subject of slavery, it is important to keep in mind that the subject matter is inherently *uncomfortable*. It will be uncomfortable for staff and visitors. Successful training in this context requires a shift from the idea of creating interpreter comfort with content to developing confidence and competence to manage the subject. As with all interpretation, providing research, documentation, and a strong grounding in the larger context of the content produces interpreter competence with the subject matter and the confidence to respond to a wide array of visitor questions. Successful training to discuss slavery, however, also depends on developing interpreter confidence with the understanding of their own emotions around slavery and the emotions of visitors. Expectations for training should include acknowledging that it is normal to be uncomfortable with the topic, and that training will teach skills to develop interpreters who are confident and competent to manage both the information and the emotions they will encounter when interpreting this complex subject.

It's not just slavery's inhumanity that makes it a difficult subject, its legacy lives on in our continuing national struggle with race. There is no way to interpret the story of slavery without contemplating sensitive issues of today's racial divides. So, before interpreters undertake the task of addressing the history of slavery with the public, they must be prepared to examine their own personal relationship with race. As discussed in chapter 8, "Perceptions of Race and Identity and Their Impact on Slavery's Interpretation," race and identity deeply affect an interpreter's experience discussing slavery. Training exercises to build this awareness will be sensitive and personal, so it is critical to create an environment where interpreters feel safe and able to openly express their views. Start the training by providing some guidelines for discussion, such as maintaining confidentiality and respecting the perspectives of others, then ask the group to participate in establishing additional ground rules that will help them feel comfortable. It is important for discussion leaders to be able to model desired interpreter behaviors, specifically, understanding the range of participant emotions around these issues and how to work with them. To prepare for this, trainers should take time to become familiar with basic techniques for facilitating challenging dialogues. When Hildene, the home of Robert Todd Lincoln in Vermont, determined to incorporate discussion of his work with the Pullman Company into their tours, they knew this would require taking on issues of race that were prevalent in Pullman's company history. They recognized the connections between the historical and contemporary issues and knew this would at times make the conversation uncomfortable for staff and visitors. Bringing in the Tracing Center to conduct training offered staff an opportunity to talk about issues of race and raise their questions and concerns. Staff nervousness transformed into relief. In planning the training, administrators listened to staff concerns and provided a forum for airing these issues. This, along with role-playing and working collectively on scripts and responses to visitor questions, provided the tools for successfully implementing the new interpretation.[1]

Addressing fears presents another area in which training staff to interpret slavery may differ from traditional training programs. Devoting time to openly and honestly discussing concerns about visitor reactions is critical to producing confidence in interpreters and assuring them that they will develop the tools to respond competently. During training, invite interpreters to air their concerns. Make a list of the outcomes they fear, and talk about how to respond if these situations occur. Some fears may seem unlikely, but exploring each scenario, and providing concrete resources for handling concerns, gives interpreters confidence that they can manage the situation. Here are some fears repeatedly expressed:

- unintentionally insulting someone
- being confronted by someone who challenges their right to tell the story
- dealing with a visitor's unwillingness to accept the legitimacy of the interpretation
- not being supported by supervisors in telling the story
- supervisors believing visitor complaints that interpreters are biased or telling a false story when, in fact, they are following the institution's interpretive objectives[2]

Training is one of the greatest resources available in resolving staff anxieties. When discussing fears, be up-front with interpreters about their expressed concerns, many of which will almost certainly manifest. For example, it is inevitable that the interpretation of slavery will insult some visitors, and this is one of the worst fears of a conscientious interpreter who prides him- or herself on offering a productive and engaging learning experience. Reassure interpreters that training will prepare them to manage these situations.

During a training session at Monticello, staff expressed fears that ranged from visitor complaints to threats of violence. Resources available to staff for responding to the potential issues included:

Figure 7.1. Nearly complete recreation of Thomas Jefferson's "storehouse for nailrod and other iron," a significant addition to interpreting slavery at Monticello.
Source: Thomas Jefferson Foundation at Monticello.

- documentation and research on the enslaved community to support their interpretation
- institutional policies outlining the requirement to discuss the subject, providing reassurance that staff would have administration support in the event of a complaint
- availability of staff, including other front-line colleagues, management, and security, to support interpreters in carrying out their job and to protect them from potential harm from a disgruntled visitor

Exploring the Emotions of Our Relationship with Race

Often an interpreter's passion for, or strong emotional connections to, the subject of slavery provide the motivation to become a dedicated advocate for telling this story. Passion and dedication can result in excellent interpretation; however, emotional responses can also distract from interpretive objectives. Interpreters must recognize when their personal relationship with race triggers emotions that can adversely influence their reactions to visitors. Emotions can manifest as physical responses, and therefore awareness of physical signs can help interpreters identify the need to take a step back from a situation to gain perspective. The following exercise helps interpreters gain self-awareness of physical and emotional responses to talking about race. It also promotes greater understanding of visitor reactions to this sensitive topic and provides an opportunity to discuss the importance of tending to the emotional effects that telling this story can have on interpreters. To begin, split the group into pairs or groups of no more than three. Sharing with a small group affords interpreters a degree of privacy and security.

1. Have interpreters take turns sharing the memory of a time when they had a challenging encounter with race, and then ask them the following questions.

    - How did they feel at the time of their challenging encounter with race?
    - What emotions did they feel while discussing the story?
    - Did anyone notice physical responses, such as butterflies in their stomach, tension in their shoulders, or uncontrolled shaking of their hands?
    - What emotions do they think others might feel when discussing these issues?
    - Did they show the emotions they were feeling while discussing the memory, or did their tone or manner portray a different emotion?

    Some may volunteer their responses to these questions, but don't compel verbal answers from anyone. Keep a list of the different emotions and physical sensations mentioned.

2. Discuss the emotions and physical responses, or even an absence of feeling, or the feeling of being distant from the conversation. This can help them recognize when personal relationships with race exert influence. Each person should develop an understanding of how these responses influence their interactions with others. Some interpreters may be more focused and articulate, others may become angry at visitors or lose focus on their interpretation. Discuss techniques for managing emotions constructively, such as:

- sharing an experience with colleagues after a difficult tour
- engaging in physical activity, taking a walk, going to the gym or for a run after work
- offering to speak with the visitor in question separately after the tour is over. This allows time to process the situation. It also allows the visitor a way out if they are feeling uncomfortable and don't really want to further pursue the issue.

3. After training is complete, continue to provide interpreters with opportunities to discuss the emotions that are triggered by the discussion of slavery. Allow them to share their successful techniques for redirecting visitor emotions and managing their own.

Throughout training refer back to this exercise when conversation touches on the emotional effects of dealing with this story. This will help interpreters remain grounded and in touch with the emotional legacies of slavery and race, and to begin to internalize the techniques they've learned.

Developing Interpreter Responsiveness to Visitors

Museum management and interpreters generally define a successful visitor experience as one where visitors emerge smiling, happy, and saying that they had fun. However, the history of slavery is a difficult one, and even visitors who are processing the experience well are likely to respond with a range of emotions and behaviors that do not fit into the typical description of cheerful, uplifting experiences. Interpreters must understand these responses and be prepared to assist visitors in processing the difficult realities of slavery and its connections to the nation's broader history.

Training must develop interpreter competence and confidence for reading the audience. Visitors exhibit behaviors that are signs of their internal process for integrating the difficult history into their current body of knowledge. It's important for interpreters to learn to recognize these signs so that they know visitors haven't shut down but are still processing the information. Julia Rose's research on these behaviors is described in chapter 1.[3] In training, it is essential to discuss these behaviors and reactions with interpreters. Reactions such as giggling, asking a question that has already been answered, or challenging the information provided need to be understood not as disruptive, rude, or ignorant, but rather as normal stages in processing difficult information. In training, interpreters can learn to recognize when a visitor's questions or comments may reveal their struggle to reconcile new information with previously held beliefs. Interpreters can develop skills to transform a deeply rooted misconception into revolutionary understandings of new information. One method for achieving this is to reframe a question and direct it back to the visitor. For example, suppose a visitor asks, "How would Martha survive if she ran away and had no master to take care of her?" The interpreter could respond, "If Martha was attending to the mistress' every need, preparing her food and dressing her, how prepared do you think she was for being on her own?" When put in the position of carefully considering the issue from a new angle, the visitor often comes to their own revelation. Brainstorm with staff for other examples of scenarios using this approach.

Figure 7.2. An interpreter at the West Baton Rouge Museum explains foodways to a student in the circa 1850 slave cabin from Allendale Plantation.
Source: West Baton Rouge Museum, Louisiana.

Reading Audience Behavior

The following exercise reinforces how to understand the behaviors visitors may display and assists interpreters in identifying the signals. Staff can practice their skills for helping visitors to process difficult information at each stage.

1. Select a group of four to six interpreters. Have one interpreter role-play as the tour guide presenting an interpretation on slavery. Select another interpreter to role-play a visitor behavior in response to the interpretation presented. Identify this person secretly and do not share with the group which behavior they will represent. The other members of the group should act as interested visitors.
2. The task for the "tour guide" is to identify the behavior being portrayed and find ways to respond that help foster the visitor's processing of difficult information.
3. Following the scenario, as a group, brainstorm additional suggestions for ways to respond to other audience reactions. For example, if a visitor laughs uncomfortably

in response to something you've said, you may say to them, "I understand that this information is disconcerting, so let's talk about what makes it uncomfortable." Or, "This content can provoke a variety of reactions from people; would anyone like to share what they are feeling?"

A better understanding of visitor responses can help interpreters address and resolve situations in which the behavior of an audience member jeopardizes the experience of others in the group. Actions that once were categorized as rude, such as laughter and jokes, disagreement with the interpreter, and persistent focus on tangential elements of the story as a distraction from uncomfortable content, can be recast as a visitor grappling with difficult new information. This awareness can help interpreters recognize why judging visitor actions or admonishing visitors for "inappropriate" behavior is unproductive for the visitor in question and can escalate a situation by creating a more uncomfortable environment for the remainder of the audience. Instead, one way interpreters can keep their program on track when responding to a visitor's misplaced laughter or incredulity is by acknowledging that this is uncomfortable material and far from our modern reality, so it is natural to find it odd, unbelievable, or laughable. Others in the audience may feel insulted or uncomfortable because of the visitor's "inappropriate" response. Therefore, it is important to acknowledge that individuals respond in different ways to learning difficult history, and their responses may disturb others. This recognition also preserves the dignity of the "misbehaving" visitor and helps the entire group move past the incident.

Training should also include developing an understanding of when it is time to let go of an issue with a visitor. Interpreters must be able to assess what is at stake in pursuing the correction of a visitor's misinformation or engaging with a visitor who persists in disagreeing. Train staff to make their point and understand that when a visitor shows signs of not immediately being able to assimilate new information, it may be time to move on.[4] Interpreters should attempt to alleviate the disruption by offering to discuss the issue separately following the tour or by empathizing with the visitor's position with statements such as "that's a commonly held interpretation of the situation, though our evidence indicates differently" or "it's easy to see how that understanding developed." Interpreters must be trained not to dismiss the visitor. Not only will that further entrench him or her as an adversary, it establishes an environment in which other visitors may be reluctant to ask questions or express their thoughts for fear of being similarly dismissed.

One of the more disconcerting situations interpreters need to prepare for is an overtly racist comment. It can, in some situations, be useful to ask a visitor to repeat what they said. This can provide the chance for them to think about the statement again and realize that it was unacceptable, give them the opportunity to excuse themselves, or drop the issue. But, these can also be the cases where an interpreter needs to call on assistance from colleagues (or perhaps even security). It is crucial to not shy away from discussing this in training. A confident interpreter is one who is secure in the knowledge that support is available when needed and who understands that they are not expected to tolerate abuse or abusive language.

Handling these situations does take practice and preparation. To build interpreter competence in managing these circumstances while keeping their emotional responses under control, provide staff with opportunities to consider and practice possible responses so that they are prepared, on the spot, to evaluate the best approach for each situation.

Managing Challenging Questions and Comments

Every site has a narrative that can prompt learning crises, so be sure to include issues particular to your site in interpreter training. For example, at Monticello issues around the relationship between Sally Hemings and Thomas Jefferson can create volatile interactions. At Colonial Williamsburg, discussion of the Bray School where enslaved children were taught to read and write can challenge previously held understandings regarding literacy of the enslaved. But at Philipsburg Manor in New York, even the fact that slavery existed at all in the North can be met with shock.

Practicing responses for the most jarring remarks will help interpreters feel confident in their ability to reply to the questions and comments that most concern them. This exercise provides time to think about responses in advance and supplies interpreters with various options to prepare them.

1. Make a list of the historical content that commonly causes learning crises for visitors to your site, along with the most frequent questions and comments about that content that present a challenge for interpreters.
2. Divide the interpreters into small groups of three to four (when possible, mix groups to include both novice and experienced interpreters). Give each group two to three of these questions to discuss and develop responses that reinforce the new narrative, respectfully redirect the visitor's focus, or bring the tour back on track.
3. Discuss some of the examples with the full group. You may wish to take notes and distribute some of the best responses for use by staff.

In addition to some of the previously noted situations, the following comments and questions can be used in this exercise.

- "My great, great, great grandfather was an indentured servant and suffered more than any of the slaves here."
- "The slaves had it made. They were taken care of by their masters, and ate and dressed better than poor whites."
- "Don't you think that slavery helped African Americans advance?"
- "How could you possibly know what you are talking about?" (directed at a white interpreter)
- "Wasn't it better to be a slave in New York (or insert any northern or upper southern state) than in Mississippi" (or insert any lower southern state or Caribbean country)?
- "Was (insert name of historic owner of your site) a good master?" or "Wasn't he better to his slaves than other masters?"[5]

When staff receive questions like these they should pause for a moment before responding. In response to some of these comments or questions, interpreters can ask visitors to step back and think about their comment or the content from the opposite perspective. It's important not to ridicule or insult visitors when they ask "stupid questions" or make "ignorant comments." This can be rude and will make visitors shut down. The interpreter should keep in mind that most visitors ask questions out of genuine ignorance, not vindictiveness, and often as part of an honest internal struggle with challenging new information. Staff should be sensitive to truths in questions or comments that may on the surface seem ignorant. These are opportunities to acknowledge how mythology and popular culture exaggerate and distort realities, and then you can elaborate on the nature of chattel slavery. Support visitors' learning by giving them a moment to think about what they said and prompt them to think about their learning process.

A Careful Reconsideration of Language

Words have power. They have the power to tell an effective story that captures visitor imaginations and lead them to a deeper understanding. They also have the power to turn visitors away and shut down learning. In the context of slavery, human beings were referred to as property, chattel, bucks, breeders, and niggers, among other dehumanizing terms. Today, those words retain the power to shame, embarrass, frighten, and humiliate. In striving to create historical accuracy and help visitors to understand the systematic subjugation imposed by slavery, it is important to carefully choose language that effectively makes the point, and know how to use it without crossing the line into visitor revulsion. A vital element in training interpreters is taking a critical look at language to understand the emotions words evoke, the subconscious messages we send through our choices in language, and changes in meaning of words over time.

Raise interpreters' awareness of the impact of their words. By referring to people with generalizations, such as "the slaves" or, even worse, "the servants," vastly different individuals are lumped together, supporting a common misconception that the experiences of all slaves were the same. Compounding that problem, the latter term used alone masks the reality of their status in bondage by omitting the important distinctions between paid servants, indentured servants, and those kept in chattel slavery.

Focus interpreters on keeping enslaved people at the center of their narrative. To foster this practice, training should concentrate on using language that directs attention to the individuality and agency of the enslaved. Instruct interpreters to use terms such as "enslaved people" rather than "slaves." The word "slave" prescribes an identity, but terms like "enslaved person" emphasize slavery as a condition rather than an identity. When we hear someone speak of "the slaves who lived on this site," it is easy to lump them together as a monolithic group. When their humanity precedes their status in society, as in "the people who were enslaved on this site," we first hear their personhood, which conjures in our imaginations variety and individuality. Of course, it is just as important to provide personal details, like names, dates, and relationships with others, when any of this information is known, in order to emphasize personhood over status as property.

In recent years, other terms that are associated with the institution of slavery have come under reconsideration. "Runaway," "escape," "rebel," and "fugitive" have been criticized because they equate enslaved people with criminals. Some institutions have adopted terms like "freedom seeker," "freedom fighter," and "self-emancipated" as a way to underscore the agency of those who attempted to secure liberty.

Yes, some terms can perpetuate dehumanizing depictions of the enslaved and the denial of personhood is central to the system of slavery, but words we might find demeaning can be essential tools in inspiring profound new understandings for visitors. Work with interpreters to develop questions for visitors, asking them to dig deeper into the meanings of these terms. For example, if using the term "fugitive" in a discussion of a runaway advertisement, ask visitors to consider how they would classify a person who took this bold step in liberating themselves from bondage. They might respond with words such as "hero," "brave," or "freedom fighter." Then ask them to define the word "fugitive." Visitors may respond with answers like "escapee," "criminal," or "outlaw." By examining the definition and connotations of the word, visitors may develop a clearer understanding of the legal status of the enslaved, the risks of escape, and the ways in which language could help shape public attitudes and obscure truths about the institution of slavery.

Interpreters must be conscious of using language that gives an accurate picture of the institution of slavery while conscientiously respecting the sensibilities of twenty-first-century audiences. Therefore, it is crucial for interpreters to understand the historical uses of words, be able to explain their changing meanings to visitors, and be aware of the connotations ascribed to them by contemporary audiences. Training should encompass discussion of the associations, connotations, and definitions of the charged words visitors will encounter at your site. In a training conversation with a group of interpreters looking at the word "Negro," they revealed various perspectives on the word:

- A white interpreter born in the 1940s grew up when this was the respectful term to refer to African Americans.
- Another asked a teenage visitor to read from a historical document that included the word "Negro." When she got to the word she stopped and exclaimed in horror, "it says the N-word!"
- Others contemplated the significance of the fact that in certain periods "Negro" and "slave" were used interchangeably.

These comments remind us that visitors carry with them different perceptions of this word, one as a respectful term and another as highly derogatory. This is an opportunity to discuss how to respond to visitors who use a term that might disturb some modern sensibilities. Highlighting changing historical meanings and uses of a word is one respectful approach to educating a visitor that certain terms are no longer appropriate and at the same time address the discomfort the word may cause for others in the group. Another interpretive opportunity is to use an encounter with this word to explore the racial and hereditary basis of slavery.

To provide your interpreters with direction for using sensitive historical language, employ this guideline: restrict the use of these words to when they can be placed in historical context. That is, use this language only when encountered in primary source documents, when an interpreter can make reference to the words with prefaces such as "the common term used in 1830 was," or when using the period-specific name of something, for example, "the Fugitive Slave Act," "a Quadroon Ball," or "a runaway ad." It may seem obvious, but a critical point to address in training is that these words should never be used to refer to a visitor. Though there are some programs, such as "Follow the North Star" at Conner Prairie in Fishers, Indiana, that direct carefully chosen elements of the dehumanization of slavery at visitors to reinforce an understanding of the mortification involved in the institution, this will require extremely careful planning and training. When using first-person interpretation or role-playing, it is important to remember that the momentum of the "realism" can often spin out of proportion, as exemplified by a middle school field trip that took a horrible turn. Students participating in an Underground Railroad program at Nature's Classroom in Massachusetts were treated as runaway slaves, "The children had to hide in the woods from their 'white masters,' and the instructors later allegedly made comments such as 'Going to get the dogs to eat you,' 'You're worthless' and 'Dumb dark-skinned Negro person.'"[6] Reportedly the "N-word" was also used to refer to the students.

Connotations, Associations, and Implications

The following exercise offers an opportunity to explore the connotations of charged words related to slavery and the emotions that these words might raise for visitors. Encourage interpreters to think about words from as many different angles as possible to raise their awareness of the variety of meanings that can be ascribed to them.

1. Make a list of potentially volatile words and phrases that might appear in interpretation at your site. Write each word or set of words on its own index card.

   Examples include:
   - Slave/Enslaved
   - Master/Owner/Slave-Holder/Enslaver
   - Affair/Relationship/Mistress
   - Boy/Buck
   - Breeder/Wench
   - Negro/Black/African American

2. Hand out the cards to interpreters and ask them to consider the many different ways the words can be perceived within the context of your interpretive narrative, and then point out the general associations visitors are likely to make with that word. Have them note their thoughts on the card.
3. Discuss several of the words as a group. Be sure to bring into this discussion those words that are of greatest concern or complexity. Ask the group to share the emotions that the word elicits for them and what they imagine it may provoke in others. Discuss the different historical uses of the word and changing connotations that may impact the meanings audiences would derive from the use of the words.
4. Discuss alternate ways of expressing historical concepts to prevent conveying misconceptions. Discuss scenarios in which visitor conceptions or associations with the words can be used to expand comprehension of complex concepts.

Throughout training, cultivate an analytical approach to words by taking opportunities to explore their various implications and definitions to illuminate the powerful interpretive opportunities they offer.

Using Primary Sources and Material Culture to Introduce Multiple Perspectives

For interpreters to feel confident and competent in front of the public, it is vital to furnish them with documentary resources and research to support their interpretation. They must be equipped to examine this material from perspectives that best facilitate bringing the enslaved community to life. This may require that even experienced interpreters learn to approach documentary evidence, material culture, and decorative arts in new ways.

The best practice is to use techniques in training that reflect the interpretive style you wish staff to achieve. For example, if staff are asked to use inquiry-based interpretation, the presentation of training content should be based on inquiry methods so as to model those techniques. Training should mirror that interpretive practice.

The best interpretations of slavery do not relegate the discussion of the subject to the outbuildings of a historic site or to programing that is specifically focused on slavery. On a visit to Oatlands Plantation in Leesburg, Virginia, the guide adeptly threaded the presence of the enslaved throughout his introductory presentation on the architectural history of the mansion. When discussing architectural details and how the house was constructed, he kept the enslaved craftsmen who executed the work present in his narrative. In training staff to accomplish this, trainers need to ensure the same incorporation of the enslaved community in their delivery as they wish guides to accomplish in interpretation. Instead of presenting a training course on the architecture of the building and separate training that expounds on the lives of enslaved craftsmen, training should model the coupling of the information that interpreters are obliged to achieve.

Best practices call for incorporating the interpretation of slavery into the site narrative, but a balance between programs that place slavery in the larger context and those that offer a specific focus on the history of slavery is necessary to foster a holistic perspective on slavery. A program that focuses on slavery presented along with site interpretation that does not address the subject positions slavery as an anomaly. Its absence from the overall site narrative leaves the impression that slavery is not a significant piece of that story, and therefore any discussion of slavery is a digression from what is important. On the other hand, slavery presents an intricate history that can be challenging to understand. Comprehension of this complex story is greatly advanced by programs designed to focus on the subject as a complement to the overall narrative. It is important for interpreters to understand how these two types of programs work together and how they can direct visitors to contextualize and focus, which builds a robust understanding of slavery.

Helping interpreters deliver an integrated narrative requires reexamining how we understand objects in our collections. Our cultural tendency to attribute the historical value of an object to its owner has traditionally resulted in museums viewing objects in terms of what they can teach us about their owners. However, this practice prevents us from seeing major parts of the integrated story we are trying to tell. Museum staff often lament that one of their greatest challenges in interpreting slavery is the lack of material collections that reflect the presence of the enslaved. This perception is dependent on the belief that the furnishings, decorative arts, and material culture relied upon to interpret the main house reflect only the lives of those who legally owned the items. Therefore, to create a narrative that is inclusive of the enslaved community requires that staff "reposition possessions." This means learning to look at decorative arts and material culture collections through the lens of those who handled them, not just those who owned them. The reality is that enslaved people typically inhabited and worked in every space of the house and were part of the most intimate events that took place in a household. Material items displaying the wealth of the owners would have been used and cared for by the enslaved members of a household, which provides an opportunity to illustrate the daily lives, work, and realities of life for the enslaved. Although the mistress of the house may have been the owner of an elaborate silver tea set, for instance, it was her cook and maid who actually handled all the pieces of the set on a regular basis. They had to be educated on the appropriate etiquette of waiting on the gentry and the proper manner of cleaning and caring for silver. The presence of such a tea set in the parlor or dining room of a house provides an excellent opportunity to examine the training needed to perform their work or to explore the relationship between mistress and enslaved maid. Successful training helps interpreters recognize and utilize these opportunities to place material culture in the context of how and by whom these objects were used.

To train interpreters to see interior and exterior spaces from new perspectives, ask them to discuss activities that took place in different locations, inside and outside the house. Have them visualize how these activities were carried out and who played what role. In this way you can illustrate how using a family bedroom can explore the role of enslaved people in raising the children and parallel that with who likely took care of the children of the enslaved. Discuss dining traditions, entertaining, and the responsibilities of enslaved people in the dining room. Examine who is bathing and dressing the master of the house in his bedchamber, and explore how the relationship between slave owners and the enslaved was simultaneously intimate and distant. All of these scenarios can aid visitors in understanding the influence enslaved people had throughout the house and the realities of daily life for all household residents, free and enslaved.

Interpreters should be trained to use specific facts and details to animate an enslaved community composed of diverse individuals who were active agents in their own lives. It is often easy for interpreters to understand and present enslaved people who ran away, plotted revolts, or sued for their freedom as actively exerting control over their lives. However, it is imperative for them to also understand how seemingly ordinary activities can be interpreted to illustrate the hand individuals had in their own survival and well-being. By keeping a garden, enslaved people exercised control over their subsistence and promoted the community's spiritual and cultural survival through the maintenance of traditional foods. The exercise of this agency was not always inspirational because surviving the brutality of slavery often involved making unpleasant decisions and taking unsympathetic action. Interpreters cannot shy away from the discussion of active agency in the form of serving as the foreman who enforced the master's rules and carried out punishments in exchange for securing a degree of privilege for his family, or betraying a rebellion in exchange for freedom.

Encourage interpreters to critically examine the activities of enslaved people to help visitors gain a nuanced understanding of the lives of those enslaved.

Raise awareness of common practices that serve to obscure the presence of enslaved people in the narrative. Earlier discussion in this chapter looked at some ways this manifests through choices in language. Another misstep is the avoidance of directly acknowledging the presence of enslaved people. By using statements that vaguely allude to their presence but simultaneously make them invisible, such as "the master and his guests were served dinner," their existence is effectively erased. Instead, always mention the enslaved explicitly, naming names and incorporating specific details about individual lives wherever possible.

Names of those enslaved are often available through inventories, court accounts, baptismal records, runaway ads and wills, but other details about named individuals may be harder to obtain. Combining what may seem like meager details with a broader historical understanding of common practices of the era, and our knowledge of human nature, provides visitors with a more robust impression of the lives of the enslaved and the owners.

Our field often overlooks the fact that the same challenges of missing information and partial facts have to be overcome in the interpretation of *any* history. All interpretation, be it of mainstream "white" history or obscure stories of disenfranchised people, involves conjecture. Where objects are placed, the facts historians select to highlight in a narrative, and how we contextualize the greater influences of a time on the wider story are all examples of *our* choices that shape the messages visitors receive. Interpreters, along with administrators and other staff, need to firmly understand this fact. In many cases interpreters lack confidence in a site's narrative around slavery because of the false conception that that story is less factual than the stories of the nonmarginalized residents of a site. Reinforcing that all interpretation, regardless of the volume of specific documentation, requires filling in a series of blanks based on context and conjecture will buoy interpreter confidence in the story they are telling.

Conclusion

In telling the complicated and challenging story of slavery, it is the interpreter's role not merely to educate, but also to help visitors achieve comfort with their discomfort. This role requires that interpreters become comfortable with the historical content so that they may develop the confidence and competence to manage a narrative that produces discomfort. Interpreters must also be trained to understand the emotions that may arise so that they may be prepared to manage their own responses and to understand those of visitors. Techniques used in dialogue facilitation will be valuable to trainers while preparing interpreters for the field, and to interpreters when interacting with visitors around sensitive issues of race. Training must help interpreters understand how to strike the delicate balance between using historical language as an essential tool in conveying a clear picture of the brutality of slavery and maintaining respect for contemporary visitor sensibilities. Finally, training should introduce interpreters to new ways of analyzing documents and material culture to enable them to provide visitors with a more inclusive and robust story. Telling the story of slavery requires new perspectives on the standard site narrative, and training staff necessitates reevaluating interpretive skill sets and training approaches to accommodate the challenges presented by an often concealed and emotionally charged history.

Notes

1. Laine Dunham, telephone interview, February 20, 2014.
2. More examples of common concerns can be found in "Interpreting Slavery at National Trust Sites: A Case Study in Addressing Difficult Topics," "Embracing Controversy: Museum Exhibitions and the Politics of Change," "Interpreting the Whole House."
3. See chapter 1 for information on Julia Rose's Commemorative Museum Pedagogy. For additional information, refer to the technical leaflet by Rose, "Interpreting Difficult Knowledge," *History News* (Summer 2011).
4. For more information, see chapter 1.
5. These are some common challenging remarks from visitor comments in letters, questions asked of interpreters, or overheard conversations of visitors.
6. Editorial, "This History Lesson Went Too Far," *Hartford Courant*, September 25, 2013.

CHAPTER 8

Perceptions of Race and Identity and Their Impact on Slavery's Interpretation

NICOLE A. MOORE

EVEN THOUGH we may not be conscious of it, how we perceive ourselves and others is critical to how we frame our interpretation of slavery. As Americans, it is ingrained in us to identify as part of a racial group—such as white, African American, or Latino—but do we really understand the social construction of race, these identities we assign ourselves and each other based on the way we look, or on our ancestry, or our cultural affiliation? Racism, which exaggerates the significance of physical differences to assert the superiority of one group over others, was an ideology constructed in the sixteenth and seventeenth centuries to justify slavery. We now live in a racialized society, "a society wherein race matters profoundly for differences in life experiences, life opportunities, and social relationships."[1] Race shapes our perceptions of each other. How we, as narrators of history, are perceived by our audience, and how we perceive our audience, play a role in the delivery and reception of the narrative. The assumptions we make about one another's race affect our perceptions.

When it comes to discussing race in the United States, we are still trying to find correct ways to approach the subject. The Civil War sesquicentennial has given historians an opportunity to push the discussion of slavery forward, and some historic sites and museums have taken advantage of this period to devote programs to telling the story of the enslaved and their fight for freedom. Hollywood produced several movies that discuss slavery in some form, including the 2012 film *Django Unchained* (directed by Quentin Tarantino, a white American) and the 2013 film *12 Years a Slave* (directed by Steve McQueen, a black Briton of Grenadian descent). These films brought slavery to the forefront; however, there was controversy in some quarters over who had the "right" to direct such films and who should be able to tell the story of the enslaved.

According to historian Ira Berlin, "the history of slavery mixes with the politics of slavery in ways that leave everyone, black and white, uncomfortable and often mystified as to why."[2] Uncomfortable or not, discussions of slavery can lead to more in-depth dialogues about racial identity. Cultural studies professor Karen M. Cardozo states that "we cannot meaningfully talk about racial identity without also talking about racism" and that "acknowledging systematic racism requires unlearning deeply cherished American myths of individualism, meritocracy, and justice."[3] That acknowledgment can start at historic sites that move past the narrative of white slave owners and take an active approach to talking about the white families who lived there, and about the enslaved African Americans who lived and worked on the property.

Visitors to historic sites and museums arrive with different expectations. Some may visit historic southern plantations with images of Tara and hoop skirts in mind and ignore the out buildings that housed African Americans. Others may visit northern mansions, commercial centers, or industrial sites, and expect to find only stories of free people. Yet there are those who come to these sites looking for the narrative of the enslaved labor force and their history. These institutions employ staff to interpret that past, hoping that they are able to make connections and engage the visitors, while providing teachable moments that we hope will last a lifetime. Sometimes, however, race and racial identity can get in the way of a teachable moment.

Race and identity play a large role in how visitors and interpreters negotiate public discussions on slavery. For interpreters, it is their job to communicate with visitors about slave owners *and* the enslaved people, and it is important that visitors look to an interpreter as a trusted storyteller, no matter what the interpreter's race. However, in practice, there may often be only a polite trust between interpreters and visitors of different racial identities, but between visitors and interpreters who share a similar racial identity there can be a higher level of trust. Black interpreters, for instance, may gain an "instant credibility" from black visitors based on racial identity, rather than on an interpreter's actual knowledge and skills in interpreting slave life.

The higher-level trust that can exist between interpreters and visitors of similar race or ethnicity is often explained as resulting from "in-group bias," in which individuals who share "racial, ethnic or other salient characteristics" find that "cooperation, trust and affection are most easily developed for other members of this in-group."[4] Of the many factors that determine whether any two people will experience mutual trust, scholars find that race is the most important. For instance, 70 percent of blacks report that other blacks can be trusted, but just 23 percent report that they can trust people in general.[5] Both black and white individuals tend to be more trusting of people of their own race.[6] This phenomenon, in which people are more likely to trust someone of their own race, is especially acute in situations where learning is taking place and where issues of authority arise. Both black and white listeners, for example, say that they are more likely to believe a speaker of their own race, whether that speaker is a college professor or a preacher.[7]

What happens when interpreter and visitor are *not* of the same race or ethnicity? We have just seen that, in general, there is likely to be a lower level of trust, at least initially. There are other dangers to in-group bias: white visitors, for instance, may look to white interpreters to validate benign views regarding slavery or to avoid having to process feelings that arise while learning more about slavery.

The bias that a visitor may have toward an interpreter on account of race can be especially acute when the interpreter is black. I grant that there is little research specifically on the role of race in historical interpretation, but we do know that college and university students, for instance, are more likely to question the competence of black professors, and that black faculty members frequently experience challenges to their authority.[8] Even worse, black professors report that based on their students' preconceptions, they also tend to be quickly judged for what students perceive as any flaws in their logic or presentation, which could reinforce those preconceptions.[9] This fact is especially troubling when interpreting slavery, as visitors tend to be wrestling with what they are learning, which clashes with their preconceived notions about slavery, leading them to seek out ways to challenge the logic or sources of information on which interpreters base their statements (see chapter 1, "Comprehensive Content and Contested Historical Narratives").

One small bit of good news for black interpreters is that black professors are less likely to be assumed to be incompetent when their subject matter is related to race,[10] which presumably applies to teaching slavery or other African American history. However, the harsh reality is that nonwhite educators are especially likely to be assumed to be biased and incompetent if they are teaching a race-related subject and offer a perspective that differs from the dominant white viewpoint—a situation that, again, is especially troubling in the case of black interpreters seeking to engage visitors with views of slavery that may clash sharply with their preexisting narratives.[11] Instead of being seen as natural authorities on the subject of race in history, black interpreters may be seen as naturally biased or perceived as unqualified to interpret this subject. This, at any rate, has been the experience of nonwhite instructors teaching race-related courses in colleges and universities, especially at institutions dominated by white administrators and staff.[12]

It is the interpreter's job to break through all of these biases and create a connection with the visitor, so that they can understand, and begin to internalize, the content, regardless of who is presenting it.

When the Race of an Interpreter Matters: The Effects of Visitor Perception

"Why do you play a slave?" "Why do you keep bringing this up?" "White people can't be trusted to tell our story. They'll just try to make it sound better than it was." "Slavery just sounds better coming from someone who is black."

When it comes to interpreting slavery, as we've seen above, visitors may judge the presentation based on the race of the interpreter before any content can pass their lips. These preconceived judgments may sway a visitor's subconscious willingness to hear or reject historical information. Conversely, the race of the interpreter can be perceived as lending credibility to a historic site, or can take it away. Visitors, black and white, can be taken aback at the truthfulness of the history, but the race of the interpreter plays a large part in whether, and how, that truthfulness is digested.

Sharon Morgan, co-author of *Gather at the Table: The Healing Journey of a Daughter of Slavery and a Son of the Slave Trade*, states, "It is undoubtedly difficult for white people to observe a black person speak/enact truthfully what occurred in the past. For black people, it is hard to watch another one of us relive experiences that were so brutal and damaging to our psyche."[13] Visitors question why slavery must be discussed at all, and wonder when African Americans will "get over it."[14] Third person interpretation allows the interpreter to retain their modern identity and utilize twenty-first-century language, but it can still be hard for visitors to accept and understand the role of the interpreter as a conduit to the past. This lack of understanding can be made worse by the racial identity of the interpreter. The notion that white interpreters are looked upon as not worthy or without the proper qualifications to tell the story of slavery is a reality that must be addressed. The idea that a white person cannot be trusted to accurately interpret the institution of slavery, using third person interpretation, could stem from perceptions that some African Americans visitors have regarding how whites view slavery. By believing whites will "sugarcoat" the narrative, these visitors may use race to draw conclusions about the interpreter, and the historic site itself, before the presentation has even begun. There are also white visitors who believe that white people cannot deliver the story of slavery in the third person as well as black interpreters can. Tom DeWolf, co-author of *Gather at the Table*, states that after visiting Great Hopes Plantation at Colonial Williamsburg, he felt that the interpretation of slavery "doesn't work as effectively when white people discuss the lives of enslaved people. It's just not authentic."[15] Upon visiting Williamsburg, DeWolf was told that there would be appropriate (racially diverse) interpreters throughout the site, and he was anticipating interacting with black interpreters at Great Hopes. At Great Hopes he encountered one white costumed interpreter who was discussing the lives of the enslaved in the third person in a reconstructed slave cabin. The experience was disappointing for him.[16] His perception that the story is more "authentic" when it comes from an African American, I believe, leads to a deeper conversation about who "owns" this shared history and, in particular, about who is "allowed" to talk about the lives of the enslaved.

A common form of pushback from black visitors, against both black and white interpreters, is that none of us should be interpreting slavery because it is disrespectful to keep rehashing the past and because we should focus on the positive achievements of African Americans. On the contrary, it's important for all visitors to see what the institution of slavery was like. When a person stands where enslaved men and women stood and is confronted with the narrative, they gain a deeper understanding of that history. But that learning experience is most often improved by the presence of an interpreter, regardless of their race. As Sharon Morgan says, "Historical interpreters do a huge service because they transport us back in time as no inanimate presentation can."[17]

There are some black visitors who may understand that though a white person is interpreting "their" history, they don't have to like it and may have strong feelings against not only the interpretation but the interpreter. It can be particularly difficult for some black visitors to loosen the proverbial grip they have on the historical experiences of slaves. One African American woman told me in passing that when she visited Jamestown in Virginia with her daughter, she did not like her tour guide, because the guide wasn't black, and "how could she tell me something she knew nothing about?"[18] Similarly, an Internet commenter states, "You don't honestly think that anyone else has been interested in telling our story do you?"[19] It is interesting that both women believe that the story of slavery is a "black story," instead of a vital piece of American history, which so entangles the lives of blacks and whites that you cannot tell the story of one without including the other. It is unfair to categorize white interpreters as not being interested in telling the story of slavery or as unqualified when it comes to sharing the narrative of slavery with visitors, in the same way that it's unfair to deflect all questions about slavery to African American interpreters.

Interpreters, both black and white, who are dedicated to telling the story of slavery using third person interpretation may find it problematic that they are judged by visitors because of their race before hearing anything they have to say. We know that race is a factor in museum staffing—79.4 percent of museum staff in the United States are white, only 11.7 percent are black.[20] This statistic, though it closely matches the racial composition of the general public, reinforces a concern often expressed by historic house museums—a shortage of black staff members can complicate the interpretation of slavery. They rely on the perception that black people are seen as more credible and as telling a more affective story of slavery. Some black interpreters are often looked upon as the logical choice to give voice to enslaved people. A visitor may expect them to be a more natural, logical, and empathetic channel for the thoughts and emotions associated with being enslaved.

This dilemma can almost paralyze some sites in terms of what site directors feel they can and cannot interpret, and it stops some white interpreters from talking about slavery at all, leaving the burden of the narrative solely on the shoulders of their black counterparts. Two examples of this can be seen in the experiences of Clarissa Lynch, a volunteer interpreter at Historic Latta Plantation in Huntersville, North Carolina, and Lisa Swetnam, a staff interpreter at Historic Brattonsville, in McConnells, South Carolina. Roughly 50 miles apart, both sites were slaveholding cotton plantations.

Clarissa Lynch, an African American, has seen white colleagues become wary of the subject of slavery because visitors will argue with them and demand that the interpreter apologize for slavery. The site has worked for years to find an appropriate way to discuss slavery, relying on staff member Ian Campbell, also African American, to discuss the lives of the enslaved. The site made national news in 2009 when Campbell chose three black students on a field trip to assist in showing how field hands would carry their burlap sacks.[21] After that incident, Lynch explained, Latta's mostly white volunteer interpreters were told to be cautious about the topic of slavery, citing a passage in the volunteer manual that specifically states that these volunteers should not get bogged down on the issue of slavery. As an African American, Lynch was supported as the main volunteer interpreter of slavery, something she said she received "a little too much support on."[22] Lynch portrayed Sukey, an enslaved cook, and visually embodied what some visitors anticipate when visiting a plantation. A black woman who knew what her role was (as a cook), and here was a site willing to let her portray that role: "It was a double edge sword of sorts. I loved the fact that Latta gave me free reign to investigate and interpret the slave experience, but the flip side to that was it did not encourage the white staff and volunteers to find a way to address slavery on a deeper level."[23] Lynch notes that, although she has enjoyed interpreting Sukey's life, as a volunteer, "I'm not around enough to expand Latta's discussion of all persons that made up plantation life."[24] With adequate training, white staff and volunteers could prepare themselves to handle questions about slavery.

Lynch and I believe that Latta could benefit from learning that proper training can make a difference in how slavery is discussed on the site.

One aspect of proper training for interpreting slavery involves providing opportunities for staff and volunteers to talk about their thoughts and feelings about slavery and to let them explore together how this subject can be interpreted for all visitors. If the staff are allowed to talk openly about their feelings on the subject, it may help them work towards a more open interpretation with their visitors. This training is ideally carried out with the help of facilitators experienced in both the history and interpretation of slavery, and in how to navigate sensitive issues of race and identity today. But this is also something that sites can attempt to carry out on their own. Lynch suggests, for instance, that staff and volunteers gather all of the questions visitors have posed during tours and have a training session that addresses how they can collectively give truthful answers without sounding apologetic: "[The institution of slavery] was after all the way things were at the time. But if you can tell the story in a way that conveys the human aspect of slavery, it does more to move people beyond thinking of blacks as just a slave. Visitors will begin to see human beings with families, friends and a community."[25] Preparing staff and volunteers to have this conversation with visitors empowers the interpreters to tell the story without fear, particularly at a place such as Latta. James Latta owned thirty-three slaves, but it is the life of Sukey, the cook, that is the one best understood. Instead of looking at Sukey as just an enslaved cook, the site could interpret Sukey's history with the Latta family, exploring what her family life was like, and what the community looked like for those thirty-three men, women, and children. For white interpreters who may face hostile questioning from African American visitors, by creating an approach of talking about the enslaved as people not as property, the interpreter gives visitors reason to pause and think not about the person telling the story, but about the subject of the story itself.

This training method would also work well for interpreters such as Lisa Swetnam of Historic Brattonsville. As a white interpreter, she has feelings of inadequacy and looks at herself as being less qualified to interpret slavery in the third person "because I'm white."[26] She can and has done third person interpretation discussing plantation life and the lives of enslaved people, but she says,

> Although I feel fairly confident that the information I present is accurate, I feel inclined to defer to an African American interpreter on the subject of slavery (also presenting in third person), if someone is available. That's just a personal quirk of mine and I'm not sure it necessarily has to do with race. If I were with a cook or spinner or gardener, who I perceived to be more experienced than I am on the subject, I would want to let them field all questions on that particular topic. And an African American interpreter, by default, spends more time interpreting slavery than I do, and would be more experienced, at least in my mind.[27]

For some visitors, Swetnam's inclination could be perceived as discomfort or avoidance of a difficult topic, but at Historic Brattonsville, the interpretation of slavery or any inquiry into slave life has been and continues to be passed to the African American interpreter on staff because they are, by default, perceived as the subject matter expert.

Breaking bad habits can be hard (and depending on one interpreter to carry the interpretation of a specific group is a bad habit), but this can be corrected, as long as interpreters are willing to learn and grow. Swetnam can work through her feelings of inadequacy by shadowing her colleague, Dontavius Williams, who is the only African American interpreter on site, and by working with African American volunteers. Presenting alongside them in the third person can help Swetnam become comfortable interpreting the story of the enslaved at Brattonsville. Instead of sending visitors to African American colleagues, Swetnam can ask black interpreters questions that she may have, and listen to how they interact with visitors, to learn not only specific material but also how to engage visitors. Although some black visitors may initially perceive her as unqualified, her knowledge and experience will speak for themselves. Historic Brattonsville could hold a series of training sessions for all staff and volunteers that allow them to explore their feelings about slavery and how to interpret it and also to share advice on how to address the challenges and challenging questions that come with interpreting slavery. Acknowledging that the onus of interpretation should not rest solely on the shoulders of black staff and volunteers is just one step in making sure that the story of slavery is presented by all in a balanced manner.

The race of an interpreter should not matter, but as much as interpreters want to say it doesn't, for visitors race and identity play a large role in how slave life interpretation is received. Historic interpreters who present in the third person understand that there are some visitors who will see them as representations of the historical figures they are talking about. Trying to live up to that reality can be hard for the interpreter, and it is frustrating to know that certain visitors have preconceived ideas about what they are going to witness based upon the race of the interpreter. Staff should accept that some visitors may be looking for interpreters who display the physical attributes *the visitors* consider important in those who lived in the quarters or worked in the house. To those visitors, it may be confusing to imagine a white interpreter working in cotton fields alongside blacks. I believe that this is why black interpreters have a perceived credibility with most visitors, and why their narrative is largely accepted as fact based on the color of their skin. It's not that the interpreter is any better than their white counterpart, it's just how the visitor pictures the site historically.

When the Race of the Visitor Matters: The Effects of Interpreter Perceptions

Many white interpreters find themselves cognizant that they are telling the story of the "other," and this can affect their interpretation. At the Royall House and Slave Quarters in Medford, Massachusetts, board member and volunteer interpreter Gracelaw Simmons notes that although the majority of their visitors are white, the site "probably gets more visits by African Americans than the average colonial house museum. I hope my tours are the same for all visitors; that said, I suspect I'm more carefully objective in presenting the facts of enslaved life at our site and less likely to share my own emotional reaction to the sadness of slavery when there are people of color in a tour group. I am more aware that I'm telling their story, rather than a generic (white) American story."[28] Simmons points out one of the more common thoughts of white interpreters, namely, that they are not telling a generic story, but a specific story to a specific group, and sometimes to specific individuals. She also points out that interpreters are often taught not to share their own thoughts—"stick to the facts"—yet when the subject triggers emotions, there is value in letting visitors explore those emotions and in preparing interpreters to help them work through their feelings.

There are other challenges that white interpreters may have to overcome in order to be successful when interacting with African American visitors. A white interpreter may feel the need to overcompensate in presenting the story of slavery to African American visitors, because they fear these visitors will assume a white interpreter doesn't appreciate the importance of the history or its legacy. Chris Barr, of the Andersonville National Historic Site, shares that he "might feel a need to push the story of slavery harder to a black family to show that their history matters, when the family might otherwise be wary of a white person's interpretation."[29]

Tommy McMorris, group tours administrator at West Baton Rouge Museum in Louisiana, notes that "coming into a tour, both you and the visitor have life experiences, including those that are based on your racial identity that shape your opinions and your view of the world. While my job as tour guide is to try and put those preconceived notions aside to give the most objective tour, the visitor doesn't have that obligation. I have to find a way to pull them into the story and really engage them in order to create a healthy learning environment."[30] McMorris pulls the visitor in by changing his method of approaching the topic of slavery based on the feedback he receives from the visitor. He realizes that this feedback is usually filtered by the lived experiences of the visitor, and often those experiences are based on the race of the visitor.[31] Once the visitor is engaged, interpretation becomes more about the story and less about the race and identity of the interpreter and visitor.

Eric Leonard, chief of interpretation and education at Andersonville National Historic Site in Georgia, finds satisfaction in interpreting to black audiences. He finds that "black visitors are more interested and more willing to have an honest discussion [about slavery and the roles of slaves at Andersonville Prison]. It makes me more confident when I am more genuinely received by black audiences when speaking about slavery. White visitors are either noncommittal, or not interested if they hail from certain geographic regions or economic backgrounds."[32] Confidence in one's interpretation is important. If interpreters are comfortable talking about slavery, visitors often perceive this, responding by asking more questions and by pushing the interpreter to share more. For some white interpreters, validation from black audiences not only confirms their work, it allows them to make a connection with visitors based on the content of their presentation instead of their skin color.

Although white interpreters may see challenges and diligently work to overcome visitor perceptions, black interpreters that I have spoken to say they make few, if any, assumptions about their visitors. It's quite possible that being black lends comfort when interpreting slavery. Physical appearance alone gives them instant credibility with visitors, making it somewhat easier for the interpreter to engage visitors in discussions about slavery.

Emmanuel Dabney, of Petersburg National Battlefield in Virginia, and Dontavius Williams, of Historic Brattonsville in South Carolina, believe that race is not a factor in delivering their interpretations. When asked if he felt that race and identity affected his delivery, Dabney said, "No." For him, "History is history. The events happened whether you discuss them or not; but to not discuss the events is a disservice to the people who lived those experiences."[33] Williams feels similarly, noting that the race of the interpreter has little to do with the presentation of historical facts. He went on to explain that some people are simply uncomfortable with talking about the issue because it is not "their" story and are therefore disconnected from the issue of slavery in general. However, this should have little to no effect on the interpretation of facts.

The experience of black interpreters with visitors can become more challenging when interpretation is presented in the first person. Mia Marie, an interpreter for the African American Historical Interpretation division of Colonial Williamsburg, has participated in many reenactment events in the first person around the United States. She notes, "I know that as soon as I wear an 1860s style dress, it will be assumed that I am a slave."[34] Those moments open up conversation, according to Marie, that allows her to dispel myths and highlight the strength and courage of enslaved women. Comments from visitors that stem from what Marie perceives as racial hang-ups can, at times, have an impact on her methods of interpretation, but she moves forward by sharing historical research with those visitors in the hope that her words will enlighten and provoke thought.

As an interpreter, I have had to combat the issues and racial hang-ups of those around me, visitors and fellow staff members alike. In particular, I have had older white male visitors demand that I go into the (reproduction) kitchen at Historic Brattonsville and make them

Figure 8.1. At Historic Brattonsville, interpreters Nicole Moore and Ryan York portray an enslaved woman receiving medical treatment from the plantation doctor for an ailment that prevents her from working in the fields.
Source: Windy Cole.

a meal, because, according to them, "that's what you're supposed to do." It amazed me that visitors would feel comfortable treating me as if I were enslaved, instead of a person participating in third person interpretation. After that experience, I became wary of older white male visitors, because I was uncertain how they saw me and what they expected. It has surprised me that in all of the negative interactions I've had with visitors, none have crossed the line into being sexually suggestive. When adults verbalize their issues and thoughts with you, it can be off-putting. As an interpreter, I've learned to shake comments off in the moment and help a visitor to understand why a comment is bothersome. But it's especially difficult to hear things like this from children. One day, while working at Brattonsville, a seven-year-old girl from England approached me and asked how much it would cost to buy me and what skills I had that made me valuable. I did not expect that dialogue, because my perception of young visitors was that they were curious about what I was doing, and whose life I was interpreting, but not that they were wondering about my worth. It's difficult to actually try to turn a moment like that into a learning experience; it takes careful training and patience to explain that even though I am dressed like a slave woman and could have possessed skills as a seamstress, cook, or handmaid, I am a modern person and not for sale. For me, there shouldn't be a difference in my interpretation based on the race of the visitor, but there is a need to adjust your presentation to address any issues visitors may have.

Meeting in the Middle and Trying to Get It Right

Historic sites or plantation museums, previously criticized for participating in the "symbolic annihilation" of African American history, have shifted their narratives to include slavery.[35] The West Baton Rouge Museum, in Port Allen, Louisiana, discusses the lives of enslaved men and women in depth at the Allendale Plantation cabins. The site currently has a specialized tour, "From Slavery to Civil Rights," that emphasizes the story of the slave community at Allendale Plantation during slavery and the local African American community after emancipation.[36] Laura Kilcer VanHuss, consulting curator of collections at Oak Alley Plantation in Vacherie, Louisiana, speaks of how the site has come to embrace the story of slavery: "Oak Alley has, over the last couple years, sought to shift its narrative by taking the interpretative position of: This is Oak Alley's History, its entire history. Prior to this shift, what was being presented was—as with many plantations—an incomplete narrative."[37] In Medford, Massachusetts, the Isaac Royall House board made the dramatic decision to highlight the central role of slavery in the site's history by changing its name to Royall House and Slave Quarters "to reflect a more accurate description of what the visitor would learn and encounter at the museum." Among other interpretive innovations, grant money was secured to "reinterpret the kitchen and kitchen chamber to more faithfully present the presence of the enslaved in the house."[38] As more sites develop exhibits and interpretive programs that reflect the lives of enslaved men, women, and children, visitors to these sites will experience the voices of those who have been silent for so long. But with the new narratives come the concerns over addressing issues of race and identity.

Interpreting slavery is not just about reciting facts or fretting over how you, as an interpreter, think the visitor feels about you because of your race. It is about the overall content, the words, and the inflection of the interpreter's voice and tone. All of these things must be carefully orchestrated for optimal reception. If an interpreter changes their presentation to suit a particular audience, this does not automatically mean the interpreter or the site is compromising the message. Instead, this is about knowing how to get through to your audience in order to have the greatest effect. Tommy McMorris, of the West Baton Rouge Museum, understands this and works to make sure his tours reflect this thought process. "I will change my method of approaching the topic of slavery depending on the feedback I get from the visitor," he says. "This feedback is filtered through their worldview, which is based on past experiences."[39] Most often, these past experiences are based on the race of the visitor, and, as a white interpreter, he finds that he has to be careful "in my phrasing, selection of words and even tone of voice while giving my tour. Reaction to the difficult history of slavery can vary widely from person to person and the language and delivery of the tour can go a long way in making the difficult history easier to absorb."[40]

It may be beneficial to keep some aspects of your presentation the same, regardless of your visitor's race, but there are clear exceptions. For white interpreters, it is important to show empathy for black visitors who may be having a hard time with the interpretation. These interpreters must be able to stand firm when confronted with accusations of softening the past, but at the same time understand that the subject matter they are presenting is the catalyst for the hurt and anger confronting them. For black interpreters, it is important to understand that there will be white visitors looking for an "out," a way to affirm their preexisting belief that slavery was not such a big deal. This resistance may come in the form of defending slave owners, using the living conditions of some slaves—brick cabins versus log cabins, for instance—as a method of proving that slavery wasn't so bad. There will also be white visitors who don't know how to deal with the emotions that come with understanding a social institution that stripped its practitioners of their humanity. Being able to calmly and resolutely handle these situations goes a long way in getting visitors to explore different viewpoints, understand pain, and look forward. A common argument I would get from white visitors looking to deny the cruelty of slavery was that "blacks were not the only ones enslaved." There are comparisons made to the oppression of Native Americans and to indentured servants, so that it wasn't just a "black versus white" thing. McMorris relates that one visitor argued the existence of black slave owners proves that race and slavery were not intertwined. There are also visitors who have broken down in tears seeing me dressed as an enslaved woman, even though my interpretation was in the third person. As interpreters, we cannot control how visitors will respond, but we can respond to them and hope that our presentations will allow them to look further.

These situations may create uncomfortable moments for both interpreter and visitor, but they can be turned around to generate a lasting takeaway. The sweeping generalization that all experiences of slavery were the same can be particularly hard for interpreters to correct. If a white interpreter tries to explain that brutality varied across plantations, and that one slave owner might have treated those they enslaved differently from another, that interpreter may be accused of sugarcoating history. If a black interpreter tries to explain that even though some white women struggled with power, they still had more agency than black women, who were subject to coerced labor and often sexually assaulted, the interpreter may be told that they are "overreacting." In instances like these, the interpreter needs to be able to break down the generalization.

Laura Kilcer VanHuss notes that the staff at Oak Alley Plantation are encouraged to shift the conversation from broad generalizations to what she calls "scholarship supported specificity," meaning that the interpreter focuses on a specific topic within slavery and as it pertains specifically to Oak Alley: "Most of the 'uncomfortable moments' for our staff occur when a visitor makes a generalizing statement or assumption. The docent is trained to first acknowledge the person's position, relate it to what they know to be accurate at Oak Alley and then raise a question of their own. By doing this, they are respecting the visitor's query or statement, and then bringing the topic to Oak Alley and fostering a conversation that can move in a positive direction." An example of this would be a discussion about the living conditions of the enslaved. A visitor may insist that they learned slaves slept on dirt floors in run-down wooden shacks; the interpreter could acknowledge that there were slaves who lived in wood cabins with dirt floors, and then compare that generalization to the specific living conditions interpreted at Oak Alley.[41] During a recent visit to Oak Alley, a fellow museum professional found the interpretive story in the house to have very little specific information about slavery and nothing specific about individual enslaved people. Throughout the house tour, the only references made to enslaved people were generalized references of types of work done by the plantation's "slaves." The recently reconstructed slave cabins, which contained text panels with important content about slave life at Oak Alley, were the only places on the plantation where enslaved people were discussed in any detail or in a humanizing way. Unfortunately, only a small percentage of those visiting the plantation actually enter the cabins, which line the allée between the museum gift shop/café and the main house.[42]

Dontavius Williams shares an "uncomfortable" experience he had in being confronted by an older black visitor who was upset with Historic Brattonsville because the site tells the story of the 139 enslaved men, women, and children who once called the plantation home. Williams says this visitor sat on the porch of the visitor center

> and refused to go on a tour of our site because he did not like the idea of our site telling the story of slavery. After further conversation with him, I realized his opinion was not necessarily his opinion but it was the opinion that had been drilled in his head since his childhood. This opinion had shaped his view of white America in a very negative way. I challenged him to take my tour and told him that if he did not learn anything or view slavery/race relations in a different way that I would pay his admission out of my own pocket.

By allowing the visitor to express his concerns, Williams was able to show respect for the visitor's views and past experiences. This method of creating a direct dialogue "gives the visitor the opportunity to work through their discomfort and hopefully make them feel comfortable and listened to," says McMorris, who also utilizes this method with his guests in Baton Rouge. "By showing respect for what the visitor has to say, the visitor will then usually become more open and accepting to other viewpoints," as was the case with Williams. By the end of the tour, the "self-proclaimed militant visitor," Williams said, "shared that my insight and the information I presented to him changed his entire perspective on the subject, and he vowed to come back and bring friends who needed to have the same reawakening that he felt."

Figure 8.2. Located on Oak Alley's historic grounds, almost exactly where the original buildings stood, six reconstructed cabins give insight into the lives of the enslaved. Four of the cabins depict historic dwellings—a field slave's quarters, a house slave's quarters, a sick house, and a postemancipation residence—and two have been converted to exhibit spaces, inviting visitors to understand slave life on a more personal level.
Source: Oak Alley Plantation.

Both McMorris and Williams utilize tools that all interpreters should be equipped with. Not only do interpreters need to have professional training that can be provided by their institutions—knowledge of the history of their site, of the larger history of slavery in this country, and training in discussing issues of race—they also need to be skilled in how to lead a discussion about slavery. McMorris is adamant on this point: "The process of training isn't everything when it comes to the interpretation of slavery. Having the right personnel is essential. Not only does it take someone with textbook knowledge and public speaking skills, it takes an affable disposition, the ability to think on your feet, to be calm in stressful or antagonistic situations and, most importantly, the ability to read your audience so you can determine the best ways to approach the difficult topics."[43]

It also helps if interpreters have a few questions readily available to ask visitors during the tour. No matter what the race of the interpreter, there will be visitors who will ask antagonistic questions just to challenge the interpretation, particularly if visitor and interpreter are not of the same racial identity. However, pausing to ask visitors if there is something they want to know more about allows them to think about the material you've just presented and ask for clarification. Asking open-ended questions such as "How would you feel, knowing that your family could be separated at any moment?" allows the visitor, no matter their race, to put themselves in the shoes of enslaved men and women, think critically about their surroundings and what those surroundings represent, and take hold of the history. Hearing the responses from visitors should, in turn, make the interpreter take note and understand how their presentation affects everyday strangers. You may not have shared past experiences based on racial identity, but at least you can create a shared experience in which you reflect on the lives of the oppressed.

As interpreters work to break barriers with visitors, it's important that historic sites also provide support for their staff. The interpreter is also working through their own discomfort, so it is important to have a safe, ideally professionally facilitated, space for them to talk about visitor interactions, how questions from visitors have made them feel, and how they feel about the history and legacy of slavery. In the February 2014 issue of *Public Historian*, Azie Dungey of the popular "Ask A Slave" Web series talked about a co-worker at Mount Vernon who had trouble judging the institution of slavery as a whole. She noted that she felt his reaction "may have been personal, from his personal family history that he was not comfortable confronting."[44] All interpreters come to the job having their own feelings about certain subjects, and slavery in particular can often make a workplace uncomfortable if not everyone feels the same way about the subject. Sites should offer the training and support to help staff build trust in each other and trust in the interpretive plan (see chapter 7, "Developing Competent and Confident Interpreters"). Not every experience will result in interpreter and visitor sharing a warm, fuzzy moment. Slavery is uncomfortable, but creating conversation around this uncomfortable topic can engage visitors in a way that they weren't expecting, especially if they had preconceived notions revolving around race. Instead of being passive bystanders, visitors become a vital part of the interpretive process.

Lessons Learned

What lessons can we learn regarding perceptions of race and how they impact interpretation?

1. The first thing we must do is to acknowledge that people arrive with their own preconceptions. Visitors have their own strongly held ideas, beliefs, and feelings. Interpreters must recognize this and help the visitor become part of the experience offered at the site. We do this in part by making sure our interpretive presentation allows room for questions and dialogue to ensure that visitors are engaged and involved in the interpretive process.
2. Sites must also provide adequate and ongoing training to all staff members so they feel confident when addressing challenging interactions with visitors. This training should (1) provide a safe space for facilitated dialogue for those staff members who struggle with finding a level of comfort with their interpretation; (2) share the latest scholarship with staff so they are aware of new trends and have a solid foundation of knowledge to strengthen their visitor interactions; and (3) bring in various workshops and guest speakers, such as our friends at the Tracing Center on Histories and Legacies of Slavery, to help staff engage with best practices for interpreting slavery.

3. Sure, it may be difficult, but try to put your own perceptions of race aside and focus on helping the visitor understand slavery and its impact not only on the early history of our country but on the United States today.

Getting visitors to understand our interpretation of slavery is one thing, but getting staff comfortable in presenting slavery is another issue. Not only does it take top-notch interpreters willing to get down and dirty to confront slavery and deliver its history truthfully and without compromise, it also takes support and proper training from their institutions. Whether at a plantation museum or a nationally recognized historic site, training on how to handle issues of race and identity, both from the perspective of the interpreter and the visitor, is imperative to a successful interpretation of slavery. The interpreter has to be at ease with issues of race and the complexities that race and identity bring about. It takes talent to transform an uncomfortable situation into a positive learning experience, without leaving the visitor feeling like they are wrong for their preconceived ideas, especially when those ideas stem from race. Certainly, interpreters must remain objective and respectful to visitors no matter their identity, but they must also remember that the visitor has no obligation to do the same for them. To acknowledge this situation and to work through it to create a teachable moment requires skill and a deep understanding of how race and identity affect not only the interpretation of slavery but also the reception of the information. Without careful guidance, interpreters are left to handle uncomfortable situations on their own—and that could lead to disastrous results. Instead, it is important that sites take steps to prepare their staff for these interactions. One of the ways to do that is to teach the interpreter how to embrace pushback from visitors and to turn that resistance into some of the better moments in their interpretation.

Embracing the varied experiences that racial identity brings to the field can only help interpreters grow and become more comfortable in presenting slavery with confidence and authority. The material may never get easier, but understanding how race has a direct effect in how the message is given and received can allow a "coming to the table moment" for both the interpreter and the visitor.

Notes

1. Michael O. Emerson and Christian Smith, *Divide by Faith: Evangelical Religion and the Problem of Race America* (Oxford: Oxford University Press, 2000), 7.
2. Ira Berlin, "Coming to Terms with Slavery," in *Slavery and Public History: The Tough Stuff of American Memory*, eds. James Oliver Horton and Lois E. Horton (New York: New Press, 2006), 3.
3. Karen M. Cardozo, "When History Hurts: Racial Identity Development in the American Studies Classroom," *American Studies* 47 (Fall/Winter 2006),171.
4. Melissa J. Marshall and Dietlind Stolle, "Race and the City: Neighborhood Context and the Development of Generalized Trust," *Political Behavior* 26 (June 2004), 127.
5. Eric M. Uslaner, *The Moral Foundations of Trust* (Cambridge: Cambridge University Press, 2002), 107.

6. Brent Simpson, Tucker McGrimmon, and Kyle Irwin, "Are Blacks Really Less Trusting Than Whites? Revisiting the Race and Trust Question," *Social Forces* 86 (December 2007), 525–52.
7. Syed Malik Khatib, "Race and Credibility in Persuasive Communications," *Journal of Black Studies* 19 (March 1989), 361–73.
8. Katherine Grace Hendrix, "Student Perceptions of the Influence of Race on Professor Credibility," *Journal of Black Studies* 28 (July 1998), 738–63; Valerie Ann Moore, "Inappropriate Challenges to Professorial Authority," *Teaching Sociology* 24 (April 1996), 202–6.
9. Moore, "Inappropriate Challenges to Professorial Authority."
10. Hendrix, "Student Perceptions." See also Maria de la Luz Reyes and John J. Halcón, "Racism in Academia: The Old Wolf Revisited," *Harvard Educational Review* 58 (Fall 1988), 427–46; Robert Staples, "Racial Ideology and Intellectual Racism: Blacks in Academia," *The Black Scholar* 15 (March/April 1984), 2–17.
11. Moore, "Inappropriate Challenges to Professorial Authority." See also Reyes and Halcón, "Racism in Academia"; Staples, "Racial Ideology and Intellectual Racism."
12. Gary Perry, Helen Moore, Crystal Edwards, Katherine Acosta, and Connie Frey, "Maintaining Credibility and Authority as an Instructor of Color in Diversity-Education Classrooms: A Qualitative Inquiry," *Journal of Higher Education* 80 (January/February 2009), 80–105.
13. Sharon Morgan, e-mail message to author, September 29, 2013.
14. James Oliver Horton, "Slavery in American History," in Horton and Horton, *Slavery and Public History*, 47. This references a quote from Frances Chapman, who argued within the essay that "slavery was not all that bad.... Blacks just need to get over slavery. You can't live in the past."
15. Thomas Norman DeWolf, e-mail message to author, September 9, 2013.
16. Ibid., September 9, 2013, and January 12, 2014.
17. Sharon Morgan, e-mail.
18. Jacynta James, e-mail message to author, July 16, 2013.
19. Comment received on www.interpretingslavelife.com/the-problem-with-it-sounds-better, July 15, 2013.
20. American Association of Museums, "The Museum Workforce in the United States (2009): A Data Snapshot from the American Association of Museums" (November 2011), 2.
21. Eric Fraizer, "Slavery Reenactment Rankles," *Charlotte Observer*, November 13, 2009. http://www.charlotteobserver.com/2009/11/13/1053519/slavery-reenactment-rankles.html (accessed October 15, 2013).
22. Clarissa Lynch, e-mail message to author, September 27, 2013.
23. Ibid., March 6, 2014.
24. Ibid., September 27, 2013.
25. Ibid., March 6, 2014.
26. Lisa Swetnam, e-mail message to author, September 29, 2013.
27. Ibid.
28. Gracelaw Simmons, e-mail message to author, September 9, 2013.
29. Chris Barr, e-mail message to author, September 5, 2013.
30. Tommy McMorris, e-mail message to author, January 9, 2014.
31. Ibid.
32. Eric Leonard, e-mail message to author, September 5, 2013.
33. Emmanuel Dabney, e-mail message to author, September 9, 2013.

34. Mia Marie, e-mail message to author, September 18, 2013.
35. Jennifer L. Eichstedt and Stephen Small, *Representations of Slavery: Race and Ideology in Southern Plantation Museums* (Washington, D.C.: Smithsonian Books, 2002).
36. McMorris, e-mail.
37. Laura Kilcer, e-mail message to author, January 10, 2014.
38. Theresa Kelliher, e-mail message to author, September 8, 2013.
39. McMorris, e-mail.
40. Ibid.
41. Kilcer, e-mail message to author, January 9, 2014.
42. E-mail message to author, June 13, 2014.
43. McMorris, e-mail.
44. Amy M. Tyson and Azie Mira Dungey, "'Ask a Slave' and Interpreting Race on Public History's Front Line: Interview with Azie Mira Dungey," *The Public Historian* 36 (February 2014), 59.

Conclusion

> When future generations hear these songs of pain and progress and struggle and sacrifice, I hope they will not think of them as somehow separate from the larger American story. I want them to see it as central—an important part of our shared story.
>
> —*President Obama, remarks at the groundbreaking ceremony of the National Museum of African American History and Culture, February 22, 2012*

AS WE HAVE laid out in the proceeding chapters, preparing an inclusive interpretation of our collective history is not to be taken lightly. The entire process of building a comprehensive and conscientious interpretation of slavery should be one of continuous dialogue among staff, between staff and board, between institution and community, and between staff and visitors. Think about how your institution will define success. What is the institutional objective for fully incorporating stories of slavery and the enslaved at your site? How will you define success through a comprehensive narrative, staff training, and visitor interactions and reactions?

A good place to start is with sound research and a foundation of comprehensive content. This content should include both your site's specific connections to the history of slavery and the broader context within which slavery can be seen as a national story that concerns all Americans, and as a story of millions of people in diverse circumstances, with a multitude of tales of survival and resistance and richly lived experiences. Anticipate that this interpretation is likely to conflict with historical narratives informing the identities of many of your staff, stakeholders, and visitors, and that it will inevitably raise unsettling issues of race that normally remain beneath the surface at museums and historic sites. Prepare a process for managing the learning crisis that can arise when historical narratives are brought into conflict and for navigating complex issues of race and racial identity.

The process for preparing staff and stakeholders should ideally include ample historical content for context and should begin to ease participants through the very challenges of reconciling conflicting historical narratives that visitors will experience. This process should also include other elements of good interpretation, including providing space for expressions of resistance and for ample questions and dialogue throughout the difficult stages of assimilation. This training needs to include exposure to the analysis of race and racial identity in our society and robust opportunities to engage in dialogue on these issues. Facilitated dialogue, in particular, can help guide participants as they work through thoughts and feelings about race and help them gain confidence in tackling these issues openly with one another. This dialogue process can also model how interpreters can engage in discussion about the history of slavery and its legacy with visitors. Participants then can learn and practice various dialogue techniques that have proven effective with visitors. This is all part of an institution-wide training initiative that brings staff together to discuss concerns, solve problems, and allay fears in order to provide the best interpretation for your visitors.

Your interpretation will bring stories of individual suffering and agency to your visitors within the much broader context of US history. Building and sharing these narratives should bring together a wide variety of stakeholders that maintain an interest or investment in your site's history. Involving your board and the wider community in the research, training, planning, and fulfilling phases of interpretation will not only help you to develop a more robust vision of the past, but will allow you to demonstrate to your stakeholders that they matter and that their voices matter for the present and for the future.

Bibliography

THE TRACING CENTER maintains an online bibliography and resource collection for this book at www.tracingcenter.org/interpretingslavery. We welcome reader suggestions for additional material.

American Association of Museums. *Mastering Civic Engagement: A Challenge to Museums.* Washington, D.C.: American Association of Museums, 2002.

Blackmon, Douglas A. *Slavery by Another Name: The Re-Enslavement of Black Americans from the Civil War to World War II.* New York: Anchor, 2008.

Bryant, Janeen, and Kamille Bostick. "What's the Big Idea? Using Listening Sessions to Build Relationships and Relevance." *History News* 68 (Summer 2013), 3.

Buzinde, Christine N., and Carla Almeida Santos. "Interpreting Slavery Tourism." *Annals of Tourism Research* 36:3 (2009), 439–58.

Cameron, Fiona. "Transcending Fear—Engaging Emotions and Opinion—a Case for Museums in the 21st Century." *Open Museum Journal* 6 (September 2003).

Chan, Alexandra A. *Slavery in the Age of Reason: Archaeology at a New England Farm.* Knoxville: University of Tennessee Press, 2007.

Dattel, Gene. *Cotton and Race in the Making of America: The Human Costs of Economic Power.* Chicago: Ivan R. Dee, 2009.

DeWolf, Thomas Norman. *Inheriting the Trade: A Northern Family Confronts Its Legacy as the Largest Slave-Trading Dynasty in U.S. History.* Boston: Beacon, 2008.

Eichstedt, Jennifer L., and Stephen Small. *Representations of Slavery: Race and Ideology in Southern Plantation Museums.* Washington, D.C.: Smithsonian Institution Press, 2002.

Ellis, Rex. "Re: Living History: Bringing Slavery Into Play." *American Visions* (December-January 1993), 22–25.

Farrow, Anne, Joel Lang, and Jenifer Frank. *Complicity: How the North Promoted, Prolonged and Profited from Slavery.* New York: Ballantine, 2006.

Griswold, Mac. *The Manor: Three Centuries at a Slave Plantation on Long Island.* New York: Farrar, Straus and Giroux, 2013.

Horton, James Oliver, and Lois E. Horton, eds. *Slavery and Public History: The Tough Stuff of American Memory.* New York: New Press, 2006.

Katznelson, Ira. *When Affirmative Action Was White: An Untold History of Racial Inequality in Twentieth-Century America.* New York: W. W. Norton, 2005.

Lemire, Elise. *Black Walden: Slavery and Its Aftermath in Concord, Massachusetts*. Philadelphia: University of Pennsylvania Press, 2009.

Manegold, C. S. *Ten Hills Farm: The Forgotten History of Slavery in the North*. Princeton, N.J.: Princeton University Press, 2010.

Melish, Joanne Pope. *Disowning Slavery: Gradual Emancipation and "Race" in New England, 1780–1860*. Ithaca, N.Y.: Cornell University Press, 1998.

Rose, Julia. "Interpreting Difficult Knowledge." American Association for State and Local History, Technical Leaflet #255, 2011.

Shackel, Paul A. *Memory in Black and White: Race, Commemoration, and the Post-Bellum Landscape*. Lanham, Md.: AltaMira, 2003.

Simon, Nina. *The Participatory Museum*. Santa Cruz, Calif.: Attribution-Non-Commercial, 2010.

Traces of the Trade: A Story from the Deep North. 86 min. Ebb Pod Productions, 2008, DVD.

Watson, Sheila. *Museums and their Communities*. New York: Routledge, 2007.

Wilder, Craig Steven. *Ebony & Ivy: Race, Slavery, and the Troubled History of America's Universities*. New York: Bloomsbury, 2013.

Index

About the Contributors

Dina A. Bailey is the interpretation curator for the National Center for Civil and Human Rights in Atlanta, Georgia. This new institution opened in June 2014 and has a mission to empower everyone to take the protection of every human's rights personally. In fulfilling this mission, Bailey oversees four major components of the institution—interpretation/content, temporary exhibitions, educational initiatives, and community programming. Prior to working at the National Center for Civil and Human Rights, she was the director of Museum Experiences for the National Underground Railroad Freedom Center, where she oversaw the entire programmatic side of the institution. Bailey has also been a high school English teacher, teaching American literature and advanced placement English. Her degrees include a bachelor of science in middle/secondary education from Butler University; a master's in anthropology of development and social transformation from the University of Sussex; and a graduate certification in museum studies from the University of Cincinnati. Bailey has published in both the formal education and museum fields.

Patricia Brooks earned a bachelor's degree from Smith College and master's in African American history from the University of Wisconsin, Madison. She is formerly the manager of African American Initiatives at the Colonial Williamsburg Foundation, where she managed visitor programing for two historic sites and developed strategies for the interpretation of African American history across the organization. Brooks also gained valuable experience training interpreters while serving as visitor programs coordinator at the Supreme Court of the United States, where she established a volunteer docent program to deliver public education on the history and architecture of the court. Her prior experience includes mounting exhibitions and educational programs at schools and historic sites for the Prince George's County, Maryland Black History Program developing, evaluating, and implementing hands-on activities at the Capital Children's Museum; and managing archival collections at the Mary McLeod Bethune Council House, National Historic Site. She credits early experiences on school fieldtrips to places such as Plimoth Plantation, the Boston Children's Museum, and the Jackson Homestead (the historical society in her hometown of Newton, Massachusetts) with bringing history to life and sparking her love of the subject. She is currently a senior program officer with the National Endowment for the Humanities.

Richard C. Cooper is the director of museum experiences at the National Underground Railroad Freedom Center, where he oversees the development and presentation of the overall interpretive and educational strategies used with the general public in the museum, including guided tours, demonstrations, self-guided activities, and first and third person interpretations. He also oversees the Exhibits and Collections departments at the museum. Cooper came to the Freedom Center in the capacity of the interpretive services coordinator, where he was in charge of maintaining the day-to-day operations of the Interpretive Services program within the museum's 150,000-square-foot facility that opened in 2004. He received his bachelor's in American history from the University of Cincinnati and his master's in public history from Northern Kentucky University.

Kristin L. Gallas, a public history/interpretation consultant with the Tracing Center on Histories and Legacies of Slavery, facilitates the center's workshops for public history professionals and speaks regularly at conferences, museums, and historic sites. She and co-editor James DeWolf Perry spent four years researching and developing a framework for this book—a comprehensive and conscientious interpretation of slavery at historic sites and museums. Gallas earned her master's in museum education at George Washington University and her bachelor's in secondary history education and theater from the University of Vermont. For more than twenty years she has worked in education and interpretation at historic sites and museums, including Shelburne Museum; Decatur House, the National Trust for Historic Preservation; the Montana Historical Society; and the USS *Constitution* Museum, where she developed programs, interpretation, and exhibits on a wide variety of topics. She is currently the project manager for Educational Development at the Tsongas Industrial History Center in Lowell, Massachusetts.

Conny Graft is a consultant in interpretive planning, research, and evaluation for nonprofits, including museums, parks, zoos, and health care organizations. Graft began consulting with nonprofits in 2000. In 2010, she retired from the Colonial Williamsburg Foundation, where she worked for twenty-seven years. During her time there she served in several different roles, including director of interpretive planning, director of interpretive education, and director of research and evaluation. She earned her bachelor's in American history at Bowdoin College in Brunswick, Maine. She has also participated in many workshops and webinars with the American Evaluation Association and the Visitor Studies Association. Graft has served as a consultant for many organizations, including the International Coalition of Sites of Conscience, the Smithsonian Institution, the Pew Center for Arts and Heritage, the Bronx Zoo, the American Association of State and Local History, the National Trust for Historic Preservation, and Sentara Health Care. She served as president of the Virginia Association of Museums, served on the board of the Visitor Studies Association, and was editor of the *Visitor Studies Journal*. She is a faculty member of the Seminar for Historical Administration. She is past co-chair of Visitor Voices, a discussion group for history museums interested in sharing and learning about evaluation. She has also developed webinars and workshops for nonprofits focused on how to use evaluation as a tool for planning programs. Her prime interest is in helping nonprofits build capacity to articulate and evaluate their impact and learn how to apply those insights to provide more intentional and meaningful experiences.

Katherine D. Kane, executive director at the Harriet Beecher Stowe Center since 1998, directs programs and outreach using the center's extensive collections and historic buildings. Stowe was an internationally known author and advocate, and the center uses her story to inspire social justice and positive change. The center's innovative programs include award-winning Salons at Stowe, bringing the public into the parlor for conversations around contemporary issues; and the biennial Harriet Beecher Stowe Prize for writing promoting social justice. Kane was a senior manager at the Colorado Historical Society (now History Colorado), where she worked for sixteen years, and special projects director at the Denver Art Museum. She has a bachelor's in sociology from the University of Denver, a master's in anthropology from the University of Colorado, and participated in the Getty Trust's Museum Management Institute. She has been an officer of the American Association for State and Local History, a member of the American Alliance of Museums Accreditation Commission, and is involved with several Hartford community organizations.

Nicole A. Moore, a public historian and museum professional, explores the lives of enslaved African Americans. She holds a master's in history with a public history concentration from the University of North Carolina, Charlotte. Her master's thesis, "Presenting Slavery: The Interpretation of Slavery and Its Place in Public History and at Historic Latta Plantation," examines how historic sites delivered slave life to visitors. In her current position as a museum educator for the City of Virginia Beach History Museums, develops and implements programs that educate and enlighten visitors about the history of Princess Anne County, Virginia. Prior to her work in Virginia, Moore was an interpreter at Historic Brattonsville in McConnells, South Carolina, interpreting the lives of those enslaved by the Bratton family. She worked with the Slave Dwelling Project, the Southern Discomfort Tour, and served as the project historian for the 2013 Pedal for Peace program, retracing the Underground Railroad. The 2011 National Council on Public History New Professional, Moore shares her experiences about what it's like to interpret slavery and the importance of its interpretation at historic sites and museums at www.interpretingslavelife.com.

James DeWolf Perry is executive director of the Tracing Center on Histories and Legacies of Slavery. He was nominated for an Emmy Award for his role as the principal historical consultant for *Traces of the Trade: A Story from the Deep North,* the 2008 PBS documentary about the legacy of the US North in slavery and the slave trade. Perry also appears throughout the film, as a descendant of US Senator James DeWolf of Bristol, Rhode Island (1764–1837), the leading slave trader in US history. Since the film's premiere, Perry has spoken across the nation and abroad about his family's, and the nation's, historic role in slavery, and he now leads many of the Tracing Center's public programs on racial healing and equity, including their professional workshops for educators and public history professionals. Perry attended law school at Columbia University, and his graduate work at Harvard University has included research into the transatlantic slave trade and its abolition.